Wild Orphan Friends

William J. Weber, D.V.M.

Wild Orphan Friends

PHOTOGRAPHS BY THE AUTHOR

HOLT, RINEHART AND WINSTON : NEW YORK

To Bill and John

COPYRIGHT © 1976 BY WILLIAM J. WEBER
All rights reserved, including the right to reproduce this book or portions thereof in any form. Published simultaneously in Canada by Holt, Rinehart and Winston of Canada, Limited. Printed in the United States of America
10 9 8 7 6 5 4 3 2 1

Library of Congress Cataloging in Publication Data

Weber, William J
  Wild orphan friends.

  SUMMARY: Relates stories of orphaned wild animals who are recovering from injuries and become temporary boarders with human families.
  1. Wildlife rescue—Juvenile literature.
  2. Wildlife diseases—Juvenile literature.
  [1. Wildlife rescue. 2. Wild animals as pets]
  I. Title.
  QL83.2.W42   599   76-11738
  ISBN 0-03-017536-4

Contents

Introduction 7

1 · Beauty, *a White-tailed Deer* 9

2 · Whooper, *the Tiger of the Sky* 26

3 · Violetta, *a Raccoon* 44

4 · Winky, *Another Raccoon* 57

5 · Bob, *a Bobwhite Quail* 88

6 · *Squirrels, Squirrels, Squirrels* 98

7 · *Three Barred Owls* 110

8 · Joe Nathan, *a Seagull* 122

9 · *The Friendly Otter* 137

10 · *Odds and End* 158

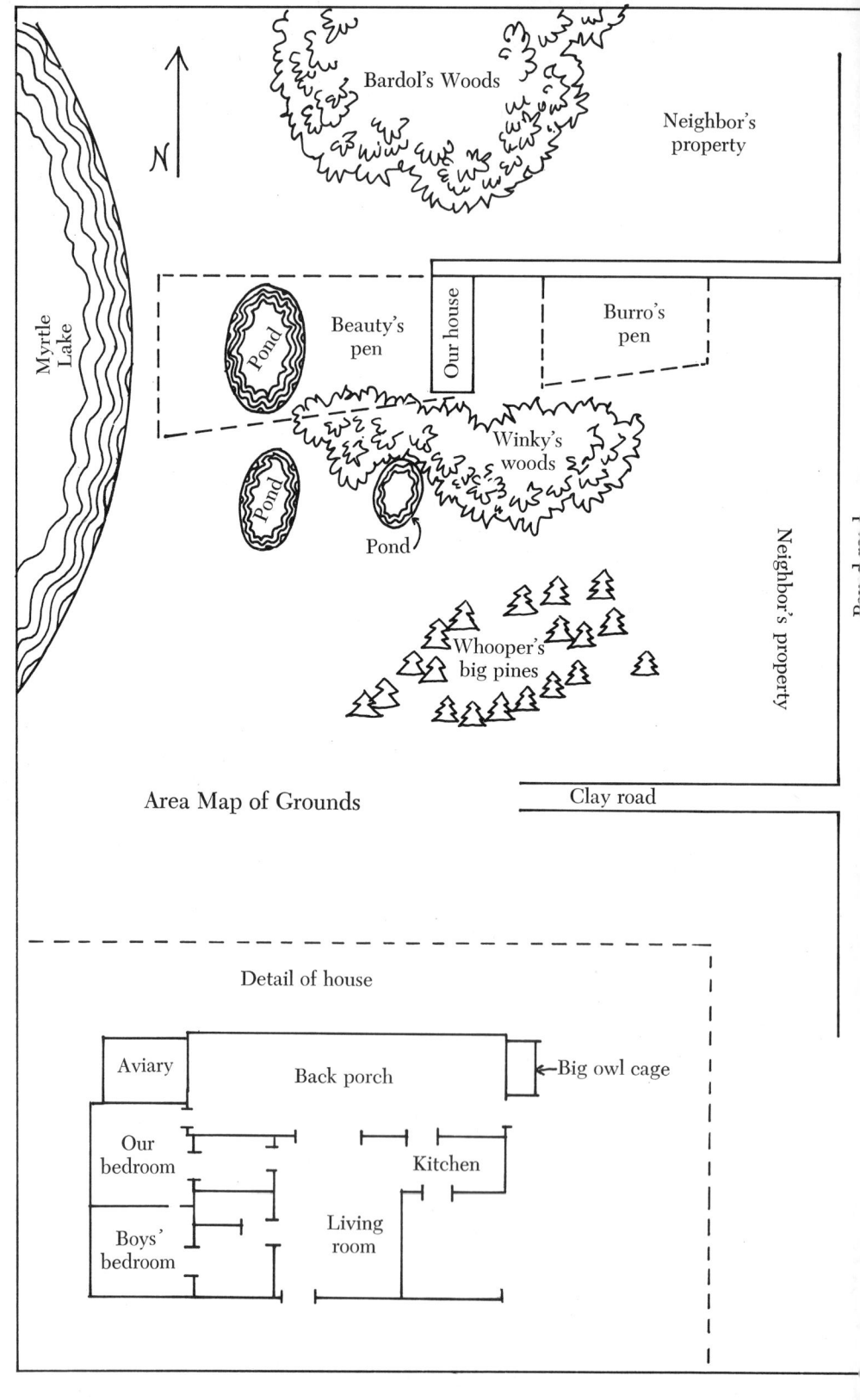

Introduction

The intention of this book is to share with you our experiences with some of the animals that have lived with us. We are the stage, or the background, for the individual stories of these creatures we—I, my wife Barbara, and our sons Bill and John—have brought to our home in Leesburg, Florida.

Our home is in the middle of a forty-acre wildlife refuge. This refuge exists because of the assistance and cooperation of our neighbors. Our 3.5 acres in the center section of the refuge are situated on the shore of a clear lake. As a veterinarian, and with the assistance of my family, we have been helping wild creatures for twenty years.

Each creature is different from the others, each has its own personality. Some we like, some we come to love. Others are so selfish and demanding, we are happy when they leave. Because the animals are such individuals, we continually encounter the unexpected.

All birds and animals have basic instinctive drives and

responses. We sometimes have made errors in judgment that bring us into a confrontation with these basic drives. Hopefully, with each encounter, we also learn. The understanding we achieve makes their visits healthier and less traumatic to them and to us.

Magazine editors accuse me of being too anthropomorphic in my writings. This means "the ascription of human feelings to something not human." I am guilty of their charge. The more I associate and work with these animals, the more convinced I am that all animals and birds display the same range of emotions we humans do. To be sure, there are limits to their expression. One would hardly expect an opossum to jump up and down with joy, but I have seen a happy opossum.

Here are only a few of the magnificent creatures we have met through the years.

WJW

:1:
Beauty,
a White-tailed Deer

It was certainly a pathetic little creature that Wildlife Officer Dennis Reese removed from the back seat of the green Game Commission car and carried into the house. Tiny, thin, with her spots showing faintly, the fawn's body was racked by convulsions. Her head was drawn back, saliva dripped from her open mouth, and all four feet pedaled aimlessly as if she were trying to flee from unknown demons.

Dennis put her on the back porch as I went for my stethoscope and thermometer. Then we laid her on a throw rug, and while Dennis steadied her head I made a quick examination.

Dennis gave me some background as I checked her. The fawn was found a month or so ago up in the Ocala scrub. The fawn was alone, her mother wasn't visible. The misguided campers, assuming the fawn was abandoned, had picked her up and brought her to the ranger station. Dennis looked at me with a pained expression in his eyes.

I knew what his expression meant.

The mother deer was probably nearby, watching them. In their ignorance, the campers stole her baby.

The officer in the area had accepted the baby deer when they brought it in, since it was too late to return it. He gave it to a couple to raise who lived on the game refuge property. They had been raising it on calf-starter formula. It was getting weaker and weaker, so they called Dennis to see if he could find help for it. And the baby was suffering from malnutrition.

To stop the convulsions, the baby needed calcium. As I prepared the injection for her, I added a little sedative to help her relax and rest.

Dennis held her head and neck still for me, and I gave the injection slowly right into the jugular vein. The calcium solution was slowly administered until the pedaling action of the legs slowed and finally stopped. I could feel the tiny body relaxing as the muscle spasms stopped.

It began to look as if she were going to make it. I gave her a tiny bit more, for good measure, then we let her rest. As I removed the needle, the little fawn rolled up onto her chest and held her head up weakly.

Dennis went back to work, promising to look in later and see how she was doing.

Bill and John, my sons, got busy converting some old carpet into a padded area for her. We all petted her and talked to her, assuring her that we meant no harm. She was so worn out from the hours of convulsions that she was too tired to be worried about us.

Barbara, my wife, fixed the fawn some formula, but the baby was too weak to nurse. An hour later she was more alert and appeared more rested. She still didn't want a bottle, though and when we tried to stand her up, she fell back. Her rubbery legs just couldn't hold her.

It was clear that she needed more medication. While Bill held her head on his lap, John steadied the little body. In a few minutes we had given more calcium by intravenous injection. The effect was almost immediate.

She was more alert, and now she wanted her bottle. She quickly polished off the eight ounces Barbara offered her. She wanted more, but that was all she was allowed right then. As she tried to grasp the empty nipple, I explained to the boys that it would be better if we gave small amounts frequently, rather than a large amount while she was still so weak.

When the boys and I stood her up on her feet, she could stand. She wobbled up to John and nuzzled his chest, looking for more food. He gently rubbed her ears and stroked her neck. "Isn't she a beauty, Dad?" he said.

"She is, and you just named her," I said. I didn't know any name that would suit her better than Beauty. The little deer wobbled up to each of us in turn. Since none of us offered her a bottle, she lay back down on her carpet. It was too bad people didn't know that deer's milk is richer than cow's milk. This never would have happened if they did.

That evening, after we fed her another eight ounces of formula, we made a little barricade to keep Beauty confined to the soft, carpeted area of the porch.

The first thing next morning, we went out to see her. The little fawn was up and waiting for us. She gave two tiny deer bleats, like the sound made by a little lamb or

Beauty takes the bottle.

goat, telling us in her own way she was hungry. That was a good sign. The way she grabbed hold of the nipple and swallowed the formula meant she was going to be all right.

She needed exercise. But the hard surface of the porch floor was too slippery for her tiny hooves. So we took her out into the back yard, where she lay on the grass, nibbled on a couple of seed heads for a few moments, then got to her feet.

She was not yet steady, but she could walk. We watched

her as she started for the woods beside the house. Instinctively the woods represented security to her. Once inside the screen of trees, she lay down and happily began nibbling on the greenbrier growing there.

After she ate, we brought her back onto the porch. But she was restless. She began to pace when we started to leave her.

Bill has a feeling for animals and understood what was bothering her. He decided, since she liked the woods so much, to bring the woods to her. He and John chopped and brought four good-sized branches, complete with leaves, and placed them in the corner of the makeshift pen.

Immediately the little deer went over to the cluster of branches, nibbled on a few leaves, and then crawled under them to lie down. As she peeked out at us, she looked truly contented for the first time since she arrived.

We set about making her feel at home. We built a six-foot-high temporary pen of chicken wire in the back yard. Approximately one hundred feet long on each side, the fence took in part of the woods, the unmowed field, and part of the lawn. Now Beauty would have natural food available to her, she would have woods for security, and room enough to exercise.

Beauty grew rapidly on her improved formula and the many additional foods offered her. After two weeks, she was normal and healthy. We enjoyed her so much we really didn't want Beauty to leave. But I felt compelled to call the Game Commission biologist for the Ocala National Forest area and report that she was fully recovered.

When he said they would stop down and pick her up one of these days, we were all depressed. But for two weeks no one came. We began to feel they had forgotten her. When another month went by and no one came for her we were relieved.

We are firm in our belief that wild creatures should have their freedom as soon as possible. But Beauty had never known the wild. Now it was too late. She could no longer be offered the freedom of the scrub. She was so people-oriented that someone would get her. I talked to the biologist from that area and told him the little deer would never make it as a wild creature. She trusted people so much that she would seek them out. As a result, she would either get hit by a car, or some outlaw would kill her. I suggested that until he could find a good place where she could be part of a wildlife exhibit or turned loose where she wouldn't get herself killed, he could leave her with us.

He agreed that it would be best if we kept her until he found the right place for her. It began to look as if Beauty would be staying for a while.

That being the case, she needed a better and bigger pen. The boys and I talked it over and agreed that she needed one at least three times as big as her present pen, one in which she could learn to find food on her own. We planned to include a couple of the big oak trees, for soon the acorns would start to drop.

We made our plans, tentatively marked out the boundaries of the new fence line, and ordered the materials. School started, and while the materials were stacked beside the garage, there just didn't seem to be time to get the pen built. Other chores came along to demand our attention. But something always happens to force us to rearrange our priorities in order to face a task we have been putting off.

That was Beauty's first escape. My bedroom window overlooks the back yard and Beauty's pen. Each morning upon waking I always looked out the window to check on the little deer.

One cool, foggy morning in September, I couldn't see her. At first I wasn't concerned. For often a deer appears to have the ability to hide behind a blade of grass. I went out on the porch to scrutinize the pen more closely. The gate was still closed, but the little deer was gone. Early-morning mists made it impossible to see beyond the limits of her fence. Hopefully she was close by.

I went back into the house and woke the boys. I explained we had to look for Beauty before they went off to school. We all dressed quickly. Bill went out into the back yard, and John and I went out the front door.

We were each going to take a different path and look in all directions. As we walked into the yard, John stopped and pointed. I looked where his finger pointed, and there in the mist, just barely visible, was the silhouette of a deer.

Three hundred yards away was our burro's pasture fence. And just beyond it the little deer stood immobile, her ears focused on us. "Beauty," I called. She took two hesitant steps toward us, her ears twitching as she moved. "Come on, Beauty," I called again.

At the second call she started toward me. She crawled under the barbwire fence which surrounded the burro pen, and with giant bounding leaps she raced toward me.

Between us was the barbwire fence that made up the near side of the pen. As she came closer she started running faster. I shouted to her, to warn her of the impending danger of the fence. Suddenly she saw it. With all four

Beauty

feet braced in a skid, she tried to stop before she hit the fence. But her momentum was too great. She was never going to make it. I cringed, visualizing the barbs biting into her skin. But instinct rescued her. Apparently she realized she couldn't stop in time. She jumped. Gracefully, she sailed over the fence. This was the first time we had seen her jump any obstacle. It was a beautiful sight.

Without a backward glance at the fence, she raced toward me. Four feet away she skidded to a halt.

She looked so proud of herself as she pranced around us. We were all relieved we had found her so easily.

She frisked around us as we walked around the house to the back yard. We tried to get her back into the pen, but Beauty was enjoying her freedom. She wanted to be with us, but she wouldn't be herded through the gate, nor would she follow us into the pen. Barbara came up with the solution. When she came out with a bottle, Beauty followed her and the bottle into the pen. She was hungry after her adventure, and the pint of formula disappeared at once.

It was after she escaped again, about a month later, that I really began to appreciate how well she could jump. On this second escape she left during the night sometime and had time enough to wander away from the house before we discovered she was gone. We found her tracks and followed them as she wandered to the other side of the lake and through another woods. We lost her trail when her tiny tracks joined those of a group of cows at a dairy farm about a mile from the house.

Our friends with horses rode the fields and woods the next two days looking for her, but no one saw her. On the third day I was elated. I found some of her tracks along the north side of the lake headed toward our house. I fully expected to see her in the yard when I got home. If not, then, she was certain to show by evening. But I was wrong. She never appeared. Perhaps I had been mistaken in the direction she had taken. Perhaps she hadn't headed for home after all.

When I awoke in the morning, I automatically looked out the window to check the deer pen. There, much to my surprise, was the little deer, walking along the fence outside her pen. Beauty was back.

I quickly woke Barbara, and while she fixed a bottle, I dashed out to the back yard. She seemed glad to see me, but not cocky and jaunty like the last time. She just looked tired and hungry. She needed no urging. This time, she went with me into her pen as I opened the gate.

Barbara brought her a bottle. Although her spots were all gone and the little deer was old enough to be weaned, she still liked her bottle at least once a day. This time she tiredly emptied her bottle, nudged each of us in turn, giving us a lick with her tongue as she did so, turned, and went to the edge of the woods and lay down. She was tired.

As we ate breakfast and discussed the latest escape we decided that a new pen had to be built at once.

The next day was Saturday. Early that morning we started putting in the metal posts that would hold the heavier, seven-foot wire of the new fence. This fence would be more permanent and much larger than her old pen. It covered about two acres of woods and fields. We had the pen over half finished when the boys and I quit working late Saturday evening.

Sunday morning the barking of a dog woke me. The sound came from the woods beyond the deer pen. Deer are instinctively afraid of dogs, so I immediately looked to see where Beauty was. As my glance swept the pen, I saw her sail over the fence.

She just seemed to float effortlessly over the old six-foot fence, clearing it by at least a foot and landing lightly on the lawn beyond. I was calling her by name as I raced out through the porch and into the yard.

She came to me at once. My presence was enough to reassure her now that the dog was moving away from us and was no longer a threat to her. She followed me willingly back into the pen. I was glad we had a full day to finish the new fence. I couldn't help but wonder if it would contain her. I knew if something frightened her enough, the way she had jumped the six-foot fence, even an eight-foot fence couldn't confine her.

At Thanksgiving time we still had the little deer, and

she was now part of the family. She could be let out of her pen when we were in the yard, and she would stay with us. She looked forward to the time we spent with her. Bill suggested that Beauty needed another deer for company. Whether he was prophetic or has the ability to have his desires granted, I am not sure, but a week later Beauty did get some company. A beautiful nine-point buck.

I got a call, telling me about him. He belonged to the Game Commission and was in a wildlife exhibit. He and another mature buck had been in a fight, and he had been badly hurt. We drove out to see him. I used a dart gun to shoot him with a tranquilizer. After he was sedated, I checked his injuries. Since his care would be involved, I decided he could best be treated at our house.

He was thoroughly groggy and offered little resistance as we loaded him in the back of my station wagon. Bill sat with him holding his antlers to prevent him from getting up and trying to jump out through a window.

The nineteen-mile ride was without incident except for the stares of passing motorists. Their faces registered great surprise when they saw the deer riding in the back of a station wagon. Several almost went off the road trying to get a better look at our passenger.

When we got home, Bill and I eased him out of the station wagon and into the deer pen. I gave him additional anesthetic intravenously, and he lay quietly while we cleaned and repaired the damage to his body. A hole in his abdomen had to be cleaned and several layers of tissue and skin had to be sutured to close the wound properly.

His lower lip and the skin of his chin had been pulled off the bone and were hanging loose. I sutured the skin back in place. After the surgery was completed, he was given antibiotics to prevent infection, and then we rolled him upright into a resting position. With his legs tucked under him and his head up, he looked like a normal deer again.

Beauty went over him thoroughly with her sensitive nose, then moved away from him. It was as if she didn't want anything to do with that big deer. He was an intruder.

We decided to name the intruder Parker. Parker was the name of the man who took care of the deer in the exhibit.

An hour later Parker could stand. As he wobbled weakly around the pen, he focused his eyes on Beauty and followed her wherever she went. Beauty might not want anything to do with him, but he certainly wanted her company.

All through December, as we treated Parker, he stayed near Beauty. She accepted him now, and they did make a beautiful picture along the lakeshore and in the woods along the back yard.

We kept Parker for some time, but when he was completely well he became dangerous. As with many male deer that are no longer afraid of people, he started challenging us when we entered the pen. He would lower his antlers and take a few steps toward us.

He surprised me the first time he lowered his antlers and moved menacingly toward me. I thought I could teach him a lesson. I had a short-handled shovel in my hand. When he was quite close, I rapped him a sharp blow on his nose.

It did not have the desired effect. I hoped that after being punished for being aggressive, he would turn and

When Parker was completely well he became dangerous.

flee. Instead it made him furious, and he charged. I saved myself by dodging behind a tree and escaping through the gate. As he lashed at the fence with his sharp antlers, I realized how frightening the whole affair had been. Once again I was all too conscious of the fact that a wild animal cannot be disciplined, and that mature animals can be dangerous.

In the weeks to come he was to threaten other members of the family. It became necessary, if we entered the pen, to carry a portable section of fence as a shield. One point was clear: before he injured any of the family, it was time for Parker to go back to the exhibit.

I sedated him with a tranquilizer dart, loaded him back into the station wagon and returned him to the exhibit. We could assure his handlers that he had all his vim and vigor again.

On the return trip home, Bill, the prophet, was at it again.

"Wouldn't it be nice if Beauty had a fawn next spring?" Parker had been with her for two months, and part of that time was the breeding season.

During the spring months there was no doubt she was pregnant. She lost her trim, streamlined shape and began to develop quite a potbelly. When her udder began to swell and showed signs of having milk in it, we knew the time was close.

On a warm May morning, at sunrise, she had a tiny fawn. She allowed us to see it the day it was born.

The baby was about twelve inches high and weighed about four pounds. It was beautiful, with big blue eyes, a tan coat, and soft white spots. Then, as wild deer do, she hid it in the tall grass.

For the next two weeks, Beauty wandered about the pen during the day and was as sociable as ever with us. But she made the fawn stay hidden. Early in the morning she would call it out of the tall grass with a soft, bleating cry, nurse it, and then send it back into the grass. Late in the afternoon she fed it again. I don't know, I never saw it, but I'm certain she fed it again at night. We seldom saw the tiny baby.

It wasn't until the baby was about three weeks old that she allowed it to come out of the tall grass and stay with her for several hours as she browsed and grazed. Already its blue eyes were changing to the brown eyes of a mature deer.

With the nourishing milk Beauty provided, the little fawn seemed to grow each day. It spent its days wherever its mother wandered. Seldom leaving his mother, the baby was shy whenever we were in the pen, and would not allow us to come close enough to touch him. There was only one possible choice for its name: Bashful.

When Bashful was a month old, he went off to explore on his own if Beauty were not active enough to suit him. He would wander into the high grass around the pond and lakeshore and through the woods sampling all the various types of vegetation.

On one of these solo trips Bashful almost died. I was working on the porch and saw him enter the high grass near the pond. It was his custom to follow a dim path that circled the sixty-foot pool of still water. I wasn't paying close attention to the fawn, although I knew he was on the other side of the pond. A scream of terror and a violent thrashing in the tall grass instantly told me where he was, and that he was in trouble.

I dashed off the porch and into the deer pen. Beauty had already raced down to the edge of the pond, but she would not enter the tall grass. Bashful screamed again. "I'm coming, Bashful," I hollered.

When I hollered, Bashful's screaming stopped. The next

Beauty and her baby, Bashful.

moment, I saw a large red fox peering at me from an open spot in the tall grasses.

When I charged at him like some enraged two-legged monster, the fox turned tail and dashed for the fence. Now free, Bashful ran around the pond to his mother.

I went up to both deer and spoke quietly to them, to reassure them. As I stroked and petted the fidgety Beauty, I could see the teeth marks on Bashful's rear leg where the fox had held him.

Bashful probably was big enough to pull away from the fox on his own without my help. And, once free, he certainly could have outrun the fox. Yet, I was glad I happened to be home and to be in a position to help the youngster escape.

As I went back to the house Barbara summed it up well when she said, "With all these animals around here, you never know what will happen next, but you can be sure there will always be something new every day."

Since that time, Beauty has had two more babies. And we have had numerous other deer temporarily share Beauty's quarters with her. Each has provided its own share of adventures.

Bashful was eventually given his freedom in a large forested reserve. Except for Beauty, the other deer will all have their freedom on the same protected reserve. Beauty's dependence upon people makes it impossible to turn her loose.

We hope Beauty will always stay with us, for she is a part of our family. We could never permit her to live the rest of her life in a small zoo-like enclosure after having grown accustomed to the semi-freedom of her large natural fenced pen. It has been over four years since she came to us, and we still enjoy her presence as much as when she first arrived.

:2:
Whooper, the Tiger of the Sky

Whooper was a baby great horned owl. The adult great horned owl is called "the Tiger of the Sky," but this soft, fluffy creature, about the size of a soft ball, did not look at all fierce. Forlorn, frightened, hungry, yes, but not fierce. John called him Whooper, and the name stuck.

He was found early on a January morning hopping along the fairway of a golf course. The golfers who found him looked around for a parent bird and a nest tree, but could find neither. One golfer scooped the week-old bird up in his cap, and the little owl finished the eighteen holes riding in the cap in the top of a golf bag and peering out over the edge. The golfers brought him to me, and I brought him home.

The tiny ball of fluff, even though he was frightened in his new surroundings, puffed up his downy feathers and tried to look fierce. As soon as we fixed him a nest in an old shoe box, he became more relaxed.

We offered him something to eat, touching tiny bits of

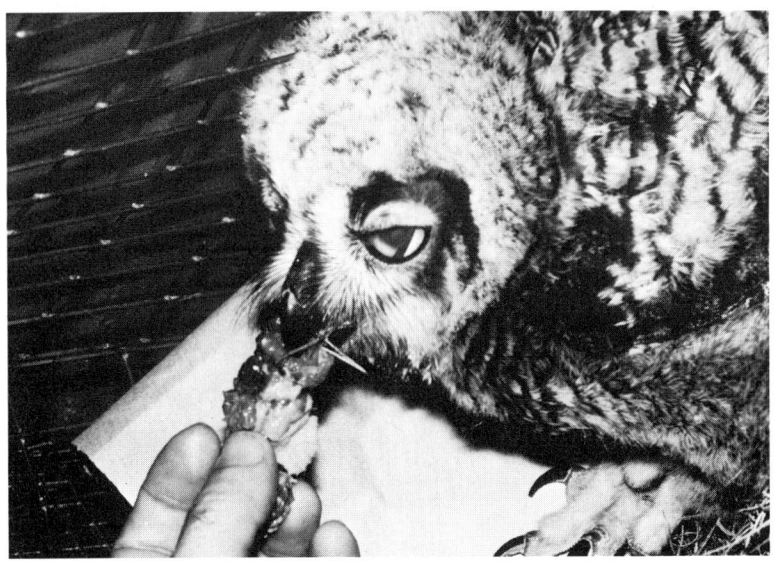

The baby great horned owl accepts a handout.

dog food mixed with egg yolk, held in my fingers, to his beak. He didn't need much encouragement. Whooper recognized it as food and grabbed for it. Most babies are difficult to teach to eat, but not this baby. He was hungry. As fast as bite-size pieces were offered, he gulped them down.

After ten bites, eyes half-closed, he lay down in his nest and took a nap. We didn't disturb him for three hours. When he woke up, he was ready to eat again.

Already he recognized us as his source of food, and welcomed us when we approached his nest. His little squeaks of pleasure, when he saw the food, became the greeting call we would come to know well.

For three weeks he was content to spend most of his time on the nest, eating, sleeping, and growing rapidly. He began to change in appearance. He was no longer the size of a soft ball, but larger than a volleyball. But he was just as round as before. We began to offer him beef heart bits as well as his dog food.

As he began to flutter to us when we came out on the porch, we knew it was time to give him larger quarters. We moved him to a six-foot-square owl cage just outside the back porch. We put numerous branches for perches around the cage and placed his nest box under the eaves where it would be protected from the rain.

He was able to jump from one perch to another at once. He tested his wings flapping from perch to perch, and he quickly learned to come to the door to be fed. We would soon be allowing him to be free part of the day for his flying lessons.

When the time came, we fed him, then opened the door of his cage. Whooper stood for a while in the doorway and looked about, not sure what he was expected to do. Then he hopped back up inside to his nest and stayed there. All afternoon he sat watching the open cage door.

The next day he was braver. After he ate, he stood in the doorway for a few moments, then fluttered to the ground. He hopped over to me and hopped up on my shoe. He sat there picking at my pants leg with his beak until I picked him up and placed him back in the cage. He was always so gentle with his beak and talons. Never once did he ever dig those sharp claws into my hand or wrist.

The following day I decided to take pictures of Whooper. After he ate, I offered my wrist and he stepped gently onto it. He was ready to go wherever I wished to take him. I took him to a nearby fence post, and he stepped off onto it. He stayed long enough for me to take a couple of pictures, then flew down to the grass.

Fear seemed to have left him. He chased and pounced upon leaves as the wind rolled them by. Seeing that he

Whooper looks about, not sure what he is expected to do.

was enjoying himself, I went around the house to work. But he followed, with the fluttering, hopping gait we would come to know so well. When he got bored watching me weed the shrubbery, he hopped off into the woods and flew up to a low limb of a little oak tree.

He sat there proudly, like a big bird, until the blue jays found him. First there was just one blue demon screaming at him and raising a clamor, darting in to peck at his big, downy head. Within minutes, the noise had attracted a dozen or more jays, who all entered the fray. The poor, bewildered little owl pulled his head down tight against his shoulders, half-closed his eyes, and was enduring the abuse when I rescued him.

He was glad to see me, and eager to get back to the security of his big cage.

By the next afternoon he seemed to have forgotten the incident and was pacing in front of his door, ready for me to let him out. This time he flew up to the top of the cage, then on to the roof of the house. For an hour he chased leaves on the roof and played in the water that had collected in the gutter after the rain.

Then he made his longest flight yet. He flew from the roof to the top of the telephone pole near the house. And there he stayed all afternoon. It was almost dark when he flew back to the oak tree near his cage.

I was afraid to leave him out all night. I climbed up the tree after him. Whooper hopped onto my wrist. I moved him to my shoulder, where he sat as I climbed back down. But he didn't seem to want to go back to the cage. As we approached it, he flew to the grass. Then he hopped back on my wrist. I talked to him for a moment, and tried to put him back into the cage, but he flew to the ground again. Exasperated, I just picked him up and put him in the cage. For the first time he threatened me by popping his beak and reaching for me with his talons.

The next day Whooper was out all afternoon. When he fussed again about going into the cage I said, "OK, you're not big enough to be on your own yet. If that red fox gets you, it's your own fault." He cocked his head, looked at me for a moment, winked, and then flew to the oak tree.

Our little owl, who had been with us for about five weeks now, was growing up.

In the morning Whooper was still up in the tree. He flew to me, and greeted me with happy, little squeaks as if to say, "See, I told you I would be OK."

From then on he never used his cage again. He moved from tree to tree in the yard. We could always tell where

Whooper, *the Tiger of the Sky* : 31

he was from the sound of the blue jays. But their raucous clamor no longer intimidated him. He seemed to enjoy the game they played.

He was fed three times a day. And three times a day one of us would call to him. If he were within hearing distance, he would "squeeek" in answer and come flying in to land at our feet.

Either John or I would feed him in the morning. He would squeak happily as he ate his beef heart and vitamins. Then he would fly off again. He would come back again in the early afternoon to be fed by Barbara. And at dusk he was fed for the last time.

After his last feeding he usually played on the roof, attacking leaves and a few old bones which had been chewed by the dogs. We could hear him hopping about when we went to bed. Sometime during the night he usually flew to one of the trees to roost till dawn.

As I went out to feed him one morning, I called him by name, as usual, once or twice. There was a squeaky answer, and he sailed directly at me with his new four-foot wing span. He never touched me with a feather, but at the last moment veered off and plopped down at my feet. I was as impressed the hundredth time he did it as I was the first time. This beautiful big bird now had his body under perfect control.

We started feeding him on the roof at dusk, because that was where he liked to play. John and I set up a stepladder so we could reach the roof to feed him. It was fun to watch him cavort around after the moving leaves, leaping high up into the air to pounce upon them.

One morning we found Whooper using the ladder for a perch. There he sat on the top step, waiting for us to come out and bring him breakfast.

If ever there was a sound of happiness, it was his squeaky greeting that morning. His voice was much more animated than usual, as if to say, "See how smart I am? You don't even have to look for me now. Here I am waiting for you." For the next week he took all his meals on the top step of the ladder. We always knew when he was there. When he wanted company or food, he would fly to the ladder and squeak his call until we heard him, and until he saw us come out.

In May, our big owl was learning the techniques of hunting. His attacks on moving leaves were practice for the real-life experience of catching food. There were mornings when he didn't act hungry. Other mornings, he was not there waiting for us at the stepladder. Those mornings I varied the routine. When I went out to feed Beauty, I took along a piece of beef heart for Whooper. If he wasn't on his ladder, I called, "Whooper." Before I reached the gate of Beauty's pen, he sailed in.

I gave him his food and went to feed Beauty. By the time Beauty had her bottle and I returned to the house, he had eaten his piece of meat. He would wait for me. I would stop beside him, and we would visit. I talked to him, and he squeaked his replies. I rubbed his beak between my thumb and index finger—and he nibbled on my hand. I scratched his chin and under his downy feathers where his ears would be. After we socialized for a couple of minutes, I went into the house for my breakfast and then left for the office.

In the evening we usually went through the same

routine. One night the family was out for the evening, and we didn't get home till 11 P.M. Whooper didn't get fed at his usual time. He had been on his own all evening. I called to him when we got home, but there was no answering squeak. When we went to sleep, there was still no sign of him.

At dawn there was a squeak. Whooper was at the bedroom window demanding breakfast. I talked to him. I hoped if I spoke to him he would be content to wait for breakfast, and I could go back to sleep. But that didn't work. Whooper continued to squeak, and insisted I get up at once. He had missed supper, so he wanted his breakfast early.

Barbara went to the refrigerator and got three pieces of beef heart for him. I lifted the screen and passed them to him, one by one. He ate one piece, then a second. The third piece fell to the ground.

Whooper left the windowsill and flew to the ground to attack the meat. At last, some peace and quiet. I rolled over and went back to sleep. But not for long. Whooper soon was back at the window and squeaking again.

Resigned to the inevitable, I got up and went to the refrigerator. There was no more heart thawed, so the hungry glutton received round steak in exchange for his silence.

Once outside, I decided to feed Beauty, too. Since Whooper had already eaten, he hopped along with me as I went in to feed the little doe. He chased leaves while I fed Beauty. Since I didn't have to hurry off to work that morning, I sat in the deer pen and visited with both Beauty and Whooper as the sun came up.

Each day we could see Whooper's soft, downy feathers

being replaced by mature feathers. His back and chest were now almost covered with the sleek feathers of a mature bird. Only his legs and head were still downy. In contrast to the sleek, mature feathers the downy areas were ruffled by the slightest breeze and always seemed to be in motion. The down flared out at his thighs, and he looked as if he were wearing puffy knickers.

Whooper stood sixteen inches tall. Except for the telltale sprouts of down on the top of his head, it was hard to think of him as a baby. Perhaps baby is the wrong word. Speaking in terms of human growth, he would be considered a teen-ager.

By the end of May all the down had been replaced by mature feathers.

One evening as Barbara went to feed Beauty, Whooper sat on his favorite limb above the deer pen, peering down at her. Usually he followed her to the door after Beauty had been fed, landing on the stepladder and waiting to be fed.

Accustomed to the routine, Barbara brought his piece of beef heart out to the ladder. But there was no Whooper. He hadn't arrived. She called, but no answer. She went back to the deer pen, thinking he was still there, but he wasn't there either.

I went out and began to call to him, but there was no answer. He would answer if he were anywhere around. He would fly to me and answer my call with his rusty, drawn-out sque-e-ek. The sound always surprised me. Now that he was almost full size and such a handsome bird, I kept expecting to hear a richer, bigger sound.

I didn't get any greeting at all any of the several times I went out that evening.

In the morning I woke early and listened. If Whooper were in the area, the crows would notify me. At daylight, as they left their roost, they came to seek him out. With the joy of mischievous boys, they harassed him with swoops, dives, and yelling until they got bored and moved on. But no crows called this morning to say they found the big gray-brown owl.

At seven I went out into the yard, fed Beauty, and called to Whooper. Cupping my ear, I listened for his squeaky response. But there was no reply.

At noon I walked the fields and woods around our house, calling occasionally. But mostly I just looked and listened. In the daytime, it was the blue jays who harassed Whooper almost continually. When the crows aren't about, they are his almost constant companions.

No harassing jays were heard, nor did I see the big, dark, familiar blob perched in any of the trees.

I was becoming concerned. It wasn't like Whooper to miss a meal. He had now missed two in a row. Had he caught his leg in a tree limb or vine? Was he caught somewhere, waiting to be rescued? Had some thoughtless hunter shot him? Had he gotten lost and sought the company and protection of humans elsewhere? What would people do if a big owl fluttered up to them? Would they kill him or accept him and feed him? All these questions gnawed at me as I worked that afternoon.

When I returned home, Whopper still hadn't showed up.

In the evening, as I fed Beauty, I watched his favorite limb, and continued to call for Whooper. I guess I expected him to appear there magically if I hoped hard enough. But by bedtime, there was still no sign of Whooper.

When he didn't show up for his evening feeding, I

crossed off the possibility of his return. Thirty-six hours with no food. Something had to have happened. Our teen-age bird could not go that long without eating.

Suddenly Barbara said, "I hear the flying squirrels squeaking their worrying cry. They really are upset. Nothing upsets them more than an owl." It was worth checking. I walked out into the night, calling, "Whooper, Whooper."

As I approached the large screened aviary where several of the flying squirrels lived, I called again. "Whooper?"

The night exploded with wings and squeaks. Whooper fluttered directly overhead and the squeaks and clicks from his beak rained over me like a summer shower. He landed at my feet and began grasping my pant leg with his beak. The constant string of squeaks conveyed the message that he was glad to be home and that he was hungry. As I rubbed his beak, he nibbled on my fingers, waiting impatiently for his food to appear.

I called to Barbara, telling her Whooper was back, and she brought out a large piece of beef heart topped with oyster shell and vitamins. Before she could place it on the ladder for him, Whooper swooped down on the food. Clicking and squeaking, he tore at the meat, consuming it in three bites.

The edge taken off his hunger, he relaxed. We got him some more food, and as we both watched, the tired, worried youngster ate, and ate, and ate. Finally he flew to the corner of the aviary to rest. The squeaks were contented squeaks now. He responded each time I spoke to him, with the lazy, contented squeak of a tired baby. He was glad to be home and wanted to go to sleep now.

In the morning, when we woke, he was on the bedroom sill looking in, waiting for us. Although he was ready to eat, he was waiting patiently, and not squeaking. Until he saw us move and heard our voices. Then he joined in with his squeaks, asking for breakfast.

The next two days he never left the yard. What adventures he experienced we will never know. We suspected, however, that something had frightened him. Whatever it was, we and he were glad that he was back. He did not go out exploring for several days.

When he began to travel again, he formed the habit of sitting on our windowsill in the morning upon his return, waiting for us to stir. We didn't mind being awakened then, usually about 6:30 A.M. We were glad to know he was all right, and that the "demons of the night" didn't get him. When we spoke to him, he squeaked a "good morning," and then flew to his stepladder to wait for his breakfast. After he had eaten and we had our morning visit, he flew across the pond to roost in the big pine trees for the day.

Each day he became more mature, more confident. By the end of June, he had lost all his down and looked like a sleek adult great horned owl. It was only when he flew back and landed in the yard in the evening for playtime that his real age showed. He was still a youngster. He enjoyed playing in the deer yard while we fed the deer and filled the bird feeders. He would attack rolling leaves or hover over a tuft of grass waving in the breeze, then drop down to plunge his talons into it. He pounced on sticks and bits of moss, and if we were close by, jumped on our shoes and untied the laces. He jumped, flew,

Whooper

hopped, tripped over his feet, and sprawled in the grass—just a big kid playing in the yard.

A gray squirrel had died stepping from the high tension line to the telephone pole. Rather than let the squirrel go to waste, I gave the squirrel to Whooper during his evening playtime. I tossed it into the grass next to him. Whooper flew up into the oak tree. He cocked his head, peered at the squirrel, looked at me, then scrutinized the squirrel again. I picked up the dead squirrel and tossed it at the base of the tree, under Whooper.

His head weaved back and forth as he looked intently at the squirrel. Then he flew down and walked around it, staring at it. Bobbing his head up and down, he circled it again. Then, like a small boy putting his toe into a cold stream, he reached one foot out, touched it with his toe, and pulled his foot back again. He walked around it once more, reached out again, and touched it more firmly with his foot.

When it didn't attack him he decided it was safe. He flew about three feet above it, hovered for a moment, and then dropped down on it as he did over the tufts of grass.

He played with it for an hour, tossing it into the air, carrying it around the yard by its tail, attacking it again and again, and eventually carrying it up into his tree.

Watching him, I felt certain he had never caught a squirrel before. But I felt he was learning to catch some prey. Although we always saw him at least once a day, he frequently did not show up at mealtime. He was not ready to be on his own yet, but it was reassuring to know that he was learning to provide for himself.

Then, one Saturday he was gone all day. He was gone

all day Sunday, too. When he didn't return on Monday, we began to worry. We walked the woods calling to him and looking everywhere for the big owl.

No answering squeaks returned our calls. That evening we reassured each other that he could catch prey—that he didn't need us any longer—but I don't think any of us were really convinced.

Tuesday night, still no sign of the big gentle owl. It had been four days now. During the evening we called every thirty minutes or so, but there was no response.

After eleven, when we had settled down for the night, I heard a squeak off in the distance, and turned on the light. "Whooper, is that you?" I said, speaking into the darkness.

A clatter of sound erupted from the night as he answered and landed on the windowsill. He squeaked, and popped his beak loudly and rapidly. Squeaking, popping, he was telling us that he was hungry and that he was happy to be home.

I got up, went out on the porch, and watched him fly over the house and land on his ladder near the door. He continued to converse with me while Barbara went to the refrigerator and got two chicken necks, two livers, and a gizzard, since no beef heart was thawed.

He practically danced up and down as he waited for something to eat. Quickly I gave him a chicken liver, then the gizzard—he swallowed them both at once. I pounded the chicken neck with the back of a hatchet to break up the bones and offered that to him. He almost took my fingers in his haste to get to it.

Then with the hungry pangs somewhat satisfied, he

squeaked and talked, without all the beak popping. I fixed the other chicken neck and offered that to him. He ate some of it and saved the rest, holding it with the long, sharp talons of his feet. We talked to him for a few more minutes and then said goodnight.

The next morning he wasn't on the windowsill, but he did come to his ladder when I went outside. He cleaned up the scraps of the chicken that remained and after talking to me for a moment, flew to the bird feeder to harass and be harassed by the blue jays.

Two gray squirrels climbed on the feeder. Although they kept a safe distance from beak and claws, they began to tease him. He ignored them.

When the crows came by on their usual early-morning rounds he flew to the top of an oak in the yard to meet them. They had come to look for him each day while he was gone. Although they harassed him with beak and voice, a swirling black mass of raucous torment, he went up to them as if to say, "See, I'm back again." He wanted to let the ornery black birds know that he was back in the neighborhood again. He took their harassment for a while, then flew closer to the house, where they were afraid to trespass. Their fear of man was greater than their desire to harass the owl.

I listened to them, glad that things were back to normal.

On July 1 we were scheduled to leave on vacation. We would be gone for six weeks, traveling and camping to Alaska and back, and Whooper would be separated from his family. So we made arrangements for Tom Rager, a student who worked for me at the office, to feed and care for all the animals. Twice a day he was to put food on the top step of the stepladder for Whooper. Whooper seemed to like Tom, and took food from him as if he were one of us.

Whenever we travel we worry about all the animals, but each year there always seems to be one we have to worry about more than the others. This year it was Whooper. I called the office every so often to check on him, and received a report on the wild creatures at the same time.

The first two weeks Tom reported that Whooper ate well, but that he was afraid of him. When he entered the deer yard, the big owl swooped down at him and pounced on his tennis shoes. Another time Whooper grabbed his pant leg in his beak, then untied his shoelaces. We laughed with Tom over the phone and explained that was the way he played. Reassured, Tom felt more at ease as he continued to care for him.

When it was time to start home and we called in for the last time, Tom told us he hadn't seen Whooper for several days. Everyone else was fine, but there was no Whooper.

I told Tom to keep putting food out for him, because he was certain to be hungry when he got back—if he did come back. I wondered, since we had deserted him, if he had left for good this time. I hoped not, for we all wanted to see him again.

When we drove into the yard around eleven o'clock at night, we received a rousing welcome. The burro brayed, the dogs barked, the ducks quacked, the chickens clucked, and the cats meowed. Best of all, from the oak tree a big owl chattered his beak and squeaked in greeting.

As we got out of the camper, Whooper flew to the ground. I scratched his chin as he nibbled on my fingers.

He visited with each of us individually, untying our shoelaces as he went. No one could have persuaded us that animals don't express emotion—that the big owl wasn't glad to see us that night.

Things at home soon settled back into their regular routine. As the fall progressed, Whooper was gone for a day or two at a time, but we stopped worrying about him. He was a big, beautiful, mature bird now and didn't really need us anymore. But he seemed to enjoy our company as we did his.

One evening during the Christmas holidays, as I was filling the bird feeder, I heard Whooper's squeak from above the roof. I looked up, and I saw him perched on the TV antenna. As I spoke to him, another great horned owl flew in out of the night and landed beside Whooper. Whooper had found a mate.

I called to Barbara and the boys, who came running. As we looked up, talking to Whooper, the other owl began to get nervous. It wasn't used to being that close to people. Whooper moved over beside it and seemed to say something reassuring in owl talk. We looked at the pair of them. Whooper was much larger than his mate. In the owl world, the female is the larger of the pair. Whooper wasn't a "he" after all. Our Whooper was a female!

The male owl flew off, and with a goodbye squeak to us Whooper followed him into the darkness.

All winter we heard them courting and calling from the big pine trees each evening at dusk. Whooper never came back to us again. We would see and hear Whooper in the distance. But she now had a new family for company and comfort. Her obligations were to them, as it should be.

:3:
Violetta, a Raccoon

Visualize this scene: You walk into your bathroom and find complete chaos. Cabinet drawers are open, and their contents scattered all over the counter and floor. Toothpaste smears are everywhere—all over the sink, cabinets, and the mirror. The well-bitten tubes, totally destroyed, lie on the floor. Lipstick smears are almost as widespread as the toothpaste. Amid all this chaos, a raccoon is sitting Buddha-like in the sink.

The little half-grown raccoon looks at you. As she lifts her hands and face toward you and gurgles happily, you see red lipstick smears on her lips and nose. Her tongue is coated with lipstick, as are her tiny, nimble fingers.

That was the scene that greeted us when Violetta was four months old.

Everyone who has raised a raccoon has similar stories to tell. Raccoons do not make good pets. Some people we know decided to keep their pet raccoon outside. They fixed it comfortable quarters just outside the door, provided food, and locked the door to keep it out. When the raccoon found he couldn't get in, he was furious. He climbed up on the roof, tore the shingles off, and threw them into the yard below. The repair bill was $200.

A veterinarian told me of visiting a farm. As he stood there talking to the farmer, he saw a raccoon walk up to the porch door, open it, enter the house, and reappear carrying a loaf of bread under one arm. The masked bandit glared at those watching him and disappeared into the nearby woods. When he asked the farmer why the raccoon was permitted to get away with it, he replied, "We don't dare stop him. Last time we locked the screen door, he pulled the screen off the door and demolished the kitchen. It's easier to just pay tribute once a day."

There are hundreds of incidents such as these. They all show why raccoons aren't good pets. On the other hand, everyone who has raised a baby raccoon enjoys it very much while the raccoon is a youngster. Each raccoon baby is an individual with its own personality. All are intriguing and appealing. The only successful way to raise them is to plan on having them return to the wild when they are mature.

When we found Violetta in the middle of the mess she had made, our first reaction was one of horror and indignation. As the little raccoon climbed out of the sink and asked to be picked up, we couldn't help but laugh at her. They are so appealing, it is easy to forgive them for acts for which they should properly be banished.

Most people acquire their raccoons in legitimate accidents, which is the way we acquired Violetta.

On a warm spring night the Blakemores, long time

clients, were sitting in their living room enjoying the soft, warm breezes that came in through the open window. Suddenly they heard a thud on the tin roof of an old shed beside their windmill.

They took a flashlight and went out to investigate. There, on the tin roof, was a tiny, hairless raccoon that had fallen some thirty feet from the gearbox at the top of the old windmill. It wasn't hurt, but was whimpering softly for its mother.

They decided to leave the baby where it was—hoping the mother raccoon would find it and take it back to the nest. To be sure that it didn't fall off the roof, they placed it in a cardboard box with shallow sides. Several times during the night they checked on the baby, but the mother did not retrieve it.

A couple of times they thought they heard more babies whimpering from a box on top of the windmill. But the windmill was old and rickety. It would have been too dangerous to try to climb up there, either to investigate or to return the baby.

In the morning the baby was still there. Mrs. Blakemore brought the baby, which appeared to be about three days old, into my office. I agreed to raise the baby and to free her when she was ready to leave.

Since the baby hadn't eaten, I took her home, fed her, and fixed her a warm nest. Once fed and warm, she seemed content and slept most of the day. Barbara named her Violetta and took over her care while I was at work and the boys were in school.

That night two more tiny raccoons tumbled out of the windmill. Hunger forced them to leave their nest and

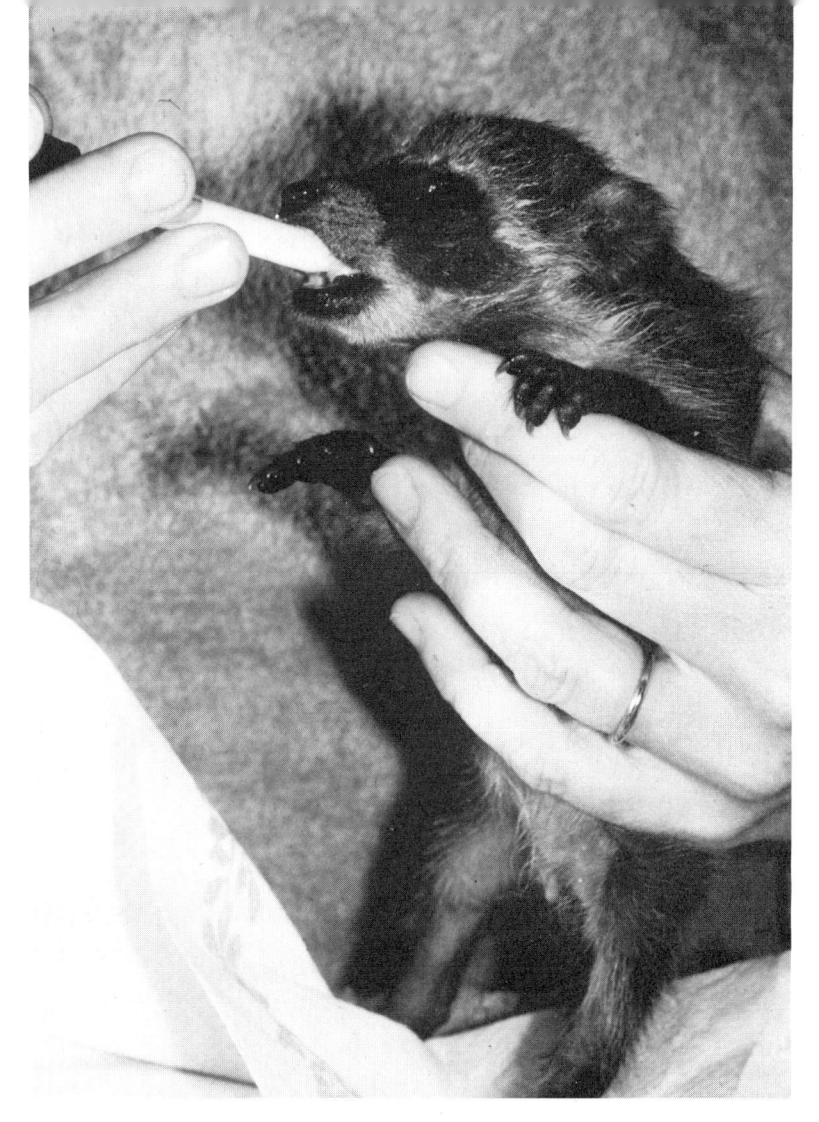

The little black mask around the eyes begins to show.

crawl out seeking their mother. The Blakemores heard the thumps that announced their arrival, went out, and retrieved two more tiny babies. They called me, and, with the assurance I would help them, they decided to raise the last two arrivals.

Our baby grew slowly, but was always healthy. After a couple of weeks she grew enough hair to allow the little black mask around her eyes to show, along with the rings on her tail. In another week her eyes began to open. This is the age that baby raccoons are the most lovable and playful. Her growth spurted, and her clumsy walk-crawl, baby gait was soon replaced with the poised balance of a young athlete.

She looked forward to her playtime with people in the evening and delighted in snuggling up in the chair with one of us. She was well housebroken, easy to care for and to feed. Her shiny black eyes twinkled with mischief as she teased the dogs and played with the boys, and her sweet disposition made her a joy to have around.

As with all babies, there are crises to weather, and this baby was no exception. The major crisis occurred when she was about ten weeks old. By this time her name had changed from Violetta, which we began to find too long, to Letta.

We had some company at the house for an anniversary party one evening. The guests had heard about Letta and insisted on seeing her.

I led them out on the porch and opened her cage and then her nest house. Instead of the usual curious raccoon scrambling into my hands, there lay a salivating, convulsing, sick baby. Froth oozed from her mouth as muscle spasms racked her body.

Many thoughts raced through my mind. Something had to have happened to her mother to make her abandon her babies. Rabies exists in the raccoon population in our area. Could this be what was affecting our baby? If the mother had rabies, she had ample opportunity to expose the babies. Had Letta acquired it from her mother's milk? What should we do?

Although there was some risk in handling this convulsing

baby, I lifted her from the nest and cleaned her where she had soiled herself. I let no one else touch her. I was the only one who had been immunized for rabies, and I didn't want anyone to be exposed.

The guests soon scattered and left us with our problem. I force-fed the little raccoon some formula. This seemed to make her feel better, but she wanted to be held and didn't want to be put back in her box. She seemed content, snuggled up to the warmth of my body. Later, when I put her back in her nest, she tried to crawl out, falling and tumbling sideways. She had lost the ability to control her muscles.

During the next thirty-six hours she gradually became more normal. She began to eat and was content to sleep in her nest box. After a week, she seemed almost to be herself again. She was once again hungry at feeding time, weakly playful, and she knew us all. While the crisis had passed, I never knew what had caused the convulsions, but it wasn't rabies.

Nevertheless, I made arrangements for the whole family to be immunized for rabies. If we as a family were going to care for wild creatures, I needed to assure myself that Barbara, John, and Bill would be protected from this most obvious risk. We all had a series of three injections of vaccine, and while the boys weren't enthusiastic, they took it like troopers.

Letta's illness didn't cause any permanent damage. She grew like a weed. She was sweet and lovable with all the family, played with Julia, our old dachshund, and in general fitted into the family very nicely.

At night we kept her in the large cage on the porch. In the daytime she was allowed the freedom of the house.

Violetta and John.

When she started weaning herself from her bottle, she began to eat dry dog food at the dog's dish. She also enjoyed "people" food that was handed her from the table at mealtimes.

She was well housebroken even as a tiny tike. We took her outdoors frequently. She would ask to go out, do her business, and then scratch to come in. If we were gone during the day and she couldn't hold out any longer, she would use the dog's water dish. Since this was not a frequent occurrence we forgave her indiscretion.

When Letta was about four months we decided to take a couple of weeks' vacation. We debated about taking her with us, but when a friend, who was experienced with wild animals, volunteered to keep her for the time that we were gone, we agreed.

Letta explored and seemed to accept her new temporary home and mistress very well. We left feeling at ease about the situation.

But the whole time we traveled and camped through

Colorado, Wyoming, and Montana, each day started with the same question. "I wonder how Letta is doing?" Even though we were reassured over the telephone, I think we were all glad to be headed home to retrieve our little masked friend.

When we picked her up and got her home I was appalled. She was literally crawling with fleas. There was only one thing to do; Violetta had to have a bath. The idea made me nervous. It was a challenge to bathe a raccoon. Anyone forcing a raccoon to do anything it doesn't wish to do often takes on a whirlwind of teeth and claws. It turned out I had nothing to worry about. Letta didn't object at all. It must have felt good to have her whole body rubbed where it itched from the flea bites. Immersed in the warm, soapy water she relaxed, lay quietly, and enjoyed her bath.

Since she was still damp, and it was late in the evening, we decided to let her stay in the house overnight. Everywhere we went, the little racoon was there. Her family had left her once before. She wasn't going to let them out of her sight to get away again. With those soft little black hands she patted our ankles or tried to crawl up in our laps if we sat down.

While we showered and prepared for bed, Letta was with us. When we got into bed she was there ahead of us in the bed and under the covers before we were. She seemed to understand that the first night home was special, and she was going to make the most of it.

Raccoons purr when they are happy and content. First she would snuggle up to me and purr; and then crawl over to Barbara and snuggle up to her and purr. The purring is louder than a cat's purr, but radiates the same contented satisfaction. Letta was enjoying being with her people too much to be able to sleep. That meant problems for us. Her purring, snuggling, and giving us soft tender pats kept us awake most of the night. She was so happy we couldn't really object or fuss at her.

The next day she had adjusted to our return. Her family was home. She went outside for short periods when she felt the need to eliminate, but kept one of us in sight at all times. She wasn't going to be left again.

That evening Letta dozed in her usual place, beside me in my chair as I read. When it was time to go to bed, I got up. Letta knew what was next. Before I could pick her up to put her outside she raced past me, jumped up on the bed, went up to the pillows, and sprawled out on her back. That little black-eyed imp lay with her head on the pillow waiting for us to join her in bed.

Barbara and I burst out laughing. She looked at us as if we were demented. Barbara pleaded for her to be allowed to stay in. But I felt she must start adapting to the outside again, or she would never be able to become a wild raccoon. We played with her for ten minutes, so her feelings wouldn't be hurt too badly when I had to put her in her cage on the porch for the night.

She whimpered softly as I carried her out on my shoulder. She wanted to stay with us. I wanted her to stay too, but she had to be ready for the next phase of adaptation to living outdoors.

Each night for the next week she would race for the bed at bedtime hoping to be allowed to stay. Each night it became easier for her to accept her old routine. After a while, when we had all settled down, the time arrived to prepare Violetta for freedom at night.

Violetta dozes on the chair.

We moved her nest box into the big cage attached to the porch outside. The cage, originally built for owls and hawks, was built three feet off the ground, so Letta would be safe from prowling dogs. The top of the cage was even with the porch roof and gave her access to the roof. A log fastened from the door to the ground made a stairway for her to reach her cage, her nest box, and her food.

Each night I put her in the owl cage when we went to bed. I gave her a few tidbits as a treat before I locked her in. In three or four days she accepted the owl cage as home, and since the door was left open during the day she could come and go as she pleased.

She scratched at the porch door when she wanted to come in, and she fussed at the door till we let her out when she wanted to be outside. She spent most of the daytime hours outside now. She was beginning to explore and forage on her own.

A raccoon instinctively sleeps during the day and forages for food at night. As they mature they are most active at night. Even though Letta was only a little over five months old she was no exception. She slept most of the day. At dusk, she was ready to visit and play. When we were ready to go to bed she was reaching her peak of playfulness.

One night as I put her in her big owl cage, I left the cage door open. She was to have her first night of freedom.

I watched from the porch as she ate her treat, a few peanuts and a couple of minimarshmallows. When she was through, she walked over to the door, as if she had just noticed it was still open. She stuck her head out the cage door and peered out in all directions. She looked at me where I stood in the darkness as if to say, "You forgot to lock the door."

When I didn't move to close it she climbed up the outside of the cage and onto the roof. During the night we could hear her scampering around up there, or playing in the gutters with pebbles from the roof. She had a wonderful time and slept most of the next day.

Each night the routine was repeated: I would carry Violetta out to her house in the cage, feed her a few treats, then go to bed. She would eat her snack, then go exploring, ranging wider and farther each night. We found her tracks all along the lakeshore and into the woods. Sometimes in the early-morning hours she would return to the cage and her house. She began to sleep every day till early evening.

She spent the evenings with us. After playing, visiting

Violetta at play.

with each of us, and finally snuggling up with one of us in the chair while we watched TV or read, she began resting up for her busy night. She was sleek and beautiful now. Our baby was growing up. Her tail had all thirteen rings, and she was as big as a grown raccoon. Each morning we checked her nest box to be sure she had returned safely and breathed a sigh of relief as a sleepy-eyed raccoon looked out at us when we called her name. In late October she moved out of the nest box in the owl cage and started sleeping under the eaves beside our bedroom window.

We have a big flight cage for injured birds that reaches almost to the roof. Letta decided that sleeping on top of the cage, where she could keep track of her people through the window, suited her. I fixed several layers of old carpeting for a bed. She made this her new home. I liked the arrangement, too. When I awoke I could glance over and see if she were back and safe.

Each morning the first thing we did was talk to her. She always acknowledged the greeting by opening her eyes to look at us, yawning, stretching, licking her lips with her little pink tongue, and then rolling over to go back to sleep.

Then in late November it happened. She wasn't in her bed when we got up. I went out and called—no response. We all went looking for her along the lakeshore and in the woods. We found some old tracks but didn't find Violetta.

We kept hoping, but each evening and morning there was no sound or sign of our baby.

The whole family was depressed for weeks. Something had happened to her—a dog, a car, a gator, a big owl. Something had taken Violetta. We tried to hope that she had found a new home, but I knew it wasn't so.

We have to keep reminding ourselves, when we raise wild orphans, that some will die, and some will be caught by predators, just the same as when raised by their natural mothers. But when we lose a baby it hurts.

It's the successes that give us the heart to try again.

:4:
Winky,
Another Raccoon

We had just returned from a vacation in late June when Betty Blakemore, who had brought Letta to us the year before, called again. Her neighbors were building a house, and the carpenters found a newborn raccoon baby in the rafters.

I suggested that she take it in for the day and then put it back where they found it in the evening. That way, if the mother came back, she could retrieve it.

Betty agreed, but made me promise that I would take it if the mother didn't come back. The two raccoons she had raised last year had caused so much damage, they had to paint the living room and buy new draperies and furniture. She and her husband were not willing to take on another raccoon.

We had enjoyed Letta so much I really wouldn't have minded raising another baby raccoon. Remembering Letta's disappearance, I thought Barbara would object. She gets very attached to each baby, and when we lose one she always says, "Never again." I knew she would weaken if I put the little baby raccoon in her hands. She always has.

I didn't mention the episode when I got home from the office. I decided to wait and see what happened.

Many people feel that if you touch any wild bird or mammal baby, the mother won't accept it after that. This isn't true. In a few cases the mother may be frightened away by the human presence, but most times they greet their babies warmly and are happy to have them back. The fact that Betty had the baby for the day would not determine whether the mother took it back or not.

The next morning I found Betty waiting for me as I drove into the office parking lot. Before I could say hello, she had plopped a warm, little, wriggling bit of life into my hands and started back toward her car.

"If I hold it for another instant, I won't be able to give it up," she said, 'and then there will be all kinds of trouble at home. I don't wish to be impolite, but goodbye. I've got to leave before I weaken."

With that she was gone and we had a new orphan to raise. I put it in my shirt pocket to keep it warm, and it went to sleep at once. When it did that I knew Betty had fed it formula before she brought it in. The new baby slept contentedly in my shirt pocket all morning while I worked, and until I could take it home at noon.

When I brought it into the house Barbara could tell I had something by the way I was smiling. I showed her the tiny baby snuggled up in my pocket. She objected, and said she wouldn't help with its care, because she didn't wish to get attached to it.

Winky, *Another Racoon* : 59

She fixed it some formula of milk with an egg yolk and a little bit of honey, and I started to feed it. When she peered over my shoulder and asked if it were a boy or girl, I knew she was already hooked. Barbara pretended to be busy with her work in the kitchen, but I could tell she was watching me. In a few moments, in spite of herself, she had to point out to me that I wasn't holding it right, so I immediately suggested she show me. Once she touched it I knew she would be hooked, so when she fell into my trap I eagerly handed the baby to her. She ate at once for Barbara, and then Barbara cuddled her and talked to her the way mothers do.

While she was doing this, I fixed up a box for the little raccoon. She was only two days old and had no fur to keep her warm. A piece of old sweater placed in a shoe box made a soft, comfortable nest, and a forty-watt bulb positioned near the nest provided heat.

After her feeding she snuggled down into her new home, and fell asleep at once. She adapted to the routine of being fed about every four hours and was an easy baby to take care of. On the third day I weighed her, and she weighed exactly one ounce.

She grew quickly and well. We got out Violetta's old cage and set it up on the porch. The new little raccoon still didn't have a name, although we had had her for three weeks. We just called her "the baby." The little black mask was distinct around the eyes, and her tail was just starting to show some rings. She weighed three ounces when her eyes started to open.

We never really try to name our babies. I guess it's because we have too many. Somewhere along the way some of them just acquire names, and this was how this little raccoon got hers.

As her eyes opened fully, one eye was a little more sensitive to light than the other. Whenever you spoke to the baby and she looked up at you, she would close her right eye and wink at you. The second time she did this she had her name: Winky. In time she stopped doing this, but the name stuck.

Winky grew fast now and wanted to be with us whenever we were home. She could hear our voices from inside the house. She would climb up the side of her cage and call with a rather plaintive two-note call that sounded more like an owl than a raccoon—"Oooh-whoo, oooh-whoo." At times it sounded as if she were saying, "Here I am, here I am." If we didn't come at once, the call became lower and very plaintive, and it seemed to us to say, "I am lost, I'm so alone." None of us could resist the plaintive "Oooh-whoo." When she called we let her out. Once she was free and in our arms; she would purr her gratitude. She was a real lover!

By the time summer was over she was getting into everything. To keep her out of the cupboards, we had to keep the doors closed with rubber bands stretched across the knobs. Every cabinet or closet in the house was fair game to her and was explored. While she was the sweetest, most lovable coon we had raised, she had a bad temper. Even as a tiny tike, we risked our fingers if we tried to pull her out of a cabinet when she once got in.

It was much easier to fix them so she couldn't open them. All the cabinets soon had some arrangement where we could lock them and keep her out. Even the bathroom

Winky makes herself at home.

cabinet drawers had to be fixed-closed or she had Barbara's curlers, combs, and make-up out. Everything she got out in the bathroom she dropped into the toilet bowl and played with in the water.

The toothbrushes had to be moved inside the medicine cabinet, for they too ended up in the toilet. The first time Barbara found her scrubbing the toilet bowl with her toothbrush, she picked her up and spanked her. Later in the day, when she came home with new toothbrushes for all of us, the humor of the situation emerged, and Winky was forgiven.

Winky was even more lovable than Letta, but this was only one of the differences. She was much more inquisitive and was always in trouble. Her bad temper made it impossible to discipline her, but she was much more intelligent.

She was perfectly housebroken even as a baby. We took her out frequently, and she seemed to know why. After she eliminated she was ready to explore. We always let her stay out as long as she liked. Even as a tiny baby she would clamber up a tree and walk out on the skinniest of limbs. If she climbed a tree, and we got tired of waiting for her to come down, we would go inside. In a little while we would hear her "Ooooh-whoo" at the door. If we didn't come at once, her call became a loud, demanding "Ooooh-whoo," as if to say, "What's the matter with you in there? Can't you hear?"

If we had to be gone for any length of time and she were left inside alone, she solved her elimination problems by using the toilet. She taught herself to go into the bathroom, position herself on the seat, and eliminate into the toilet. She was so proud of herself the first time she tried this that she called us into the bathroom with her "Oooh-whoo" to show us what she had done. We were lavish in our praise, telling her, "You're a good girl, Winky, and so intelligent. Now if you just learn to flush it, we'll have it made." But she never did learn to flush.

When she was about five months old she learned to open the back screen door and let herself in. It happened at a time when we didn't answer her "Oooh-whoo" quickly enough to suit her. She grabbed hold of the bottom of the screen door with both hands, braced her feet on the porch steps, and yanked until the latch released and the

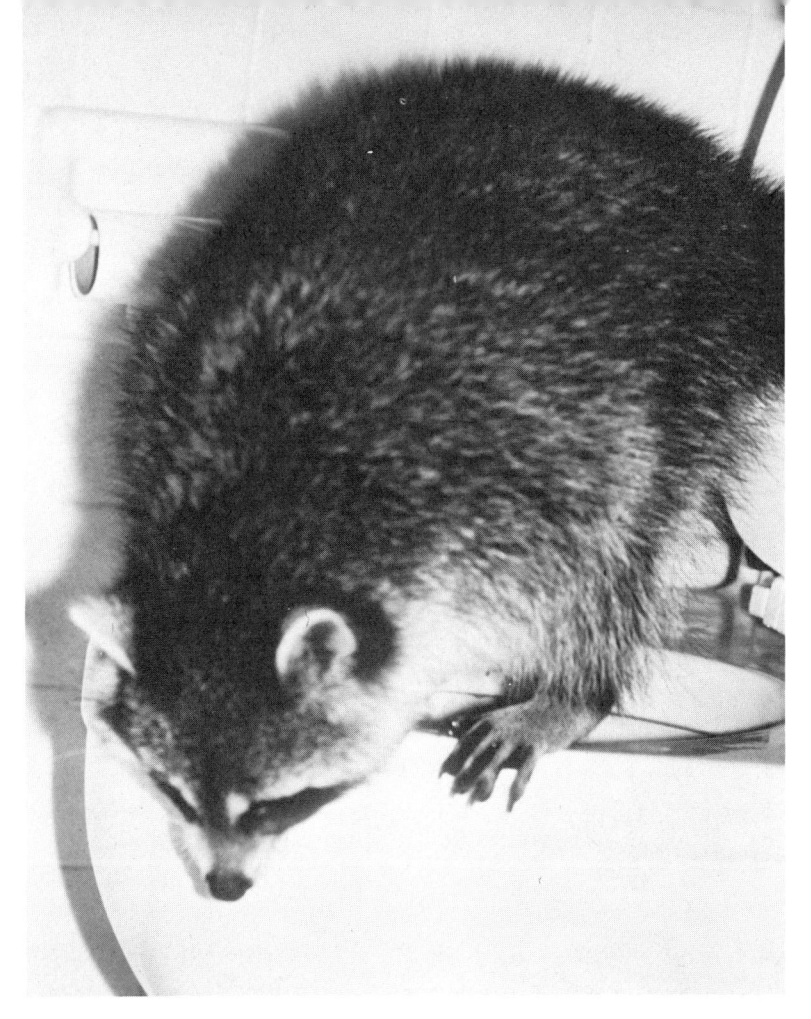

Winky taught herself to use the toilet.

door opened. We never had to open a door for her again. From then on we let her out when she indicated a desire to go out, and she let herself in.

In October I moved her nest box outside by the empty big owl cage. Each evening just before we went to bed she would go outside with me. I would put a dish of dog food by the box and, as a treat, add a couple of raisins or a minimarshmallow. She was content to be out in her cage at night. The cage door was left open.

Guided by instinct she began spending more time roaming and exploring at night. She returned to sleep in her nest box in the early-morning hours.

In September and October, as she began to wander more freely, we couldn't help but wonder if what had happened to Letta was to be repeated. So far, however, she seemed to be adapting well.

I took pictures of Winky regularly. I tried to photograph her in natural situations, such as climbing trees or fishing along the lakeshore. Early in the evening, while it was still light, I would go down to the lake. Winky would follow me. I would bait her into the position I wanted by dropping raisins in the water. She would hunt for them with her sensitive paws and seemed to enjoy the little game we played. She caught minnows and tadpoles, and was also learning to find her own food during these picture-taking sessions.

An alligator lived in our lake and during one of the picture sessions, I noticed it drifting in toward us and watching the whole procedure with interest.

That evening Barbara and I talked about that. We wondered if the gator could be the explanation for Violetta's disappearance. Then several things happened that strengthened this possibility.

One evening, instead of going to sleep in her nest box, Winky opened the screen door, came in on the back porch and scratched at our bedroom door, something she hadn't done before.

I got up, opened the door, and a furry little raccoon dashed into the bedroom, climbed up on the bed, and crawled under the covers before I could get the door closed.

Winky learns to catch her own food.

She snuggled up to Barbara, purring and patting Barbara with damp little hands, happy to be close. When I reached under the covers to bring her out, she grasped tenaciously at the sheets and cried piteously.

It was late, and I wasn't about to give a bad-tempered raccoon a lesson in discipline. Since she and Barbara were content, I went back to sleep.

In the morning we got up, but Winky stayed in bed. Barbara finally got tired of waiting for Winky to get up, and in midmorning she just went ahead and made the bed. When I came home at noon, she led me to the bedroom and showed me the bed, all made up, with a round lump in the middle.

By the time I got home in the evening, the lump had removed itself from the bed and was socializing with the family. Since it was the picture-taking evening Winky and I went outdoors and down toward the lake. She followed along happily until we got to the water.

She wouldn't go near it. She wouldn't retrieve a raisin in the shallow water. She would move up to the water's edge cautiously with that stiff-legged walk that meant she was poised for flight. She stretched her head and neck forward, and peered intently at the water. The hair along her shoulders stood straight up as she backed away from the water. I dropped more raisins into the shallow water. She wanted them, and would draw closer, but she would not enter the water. I knew that something had frightened her badly and made a lasting impression.

It was many weeks before she walked along the lake fishing for tadpoles, minnows, and all the other goodies that raccoons find there. But I never again saw her in the lake when she wasn't alert and apprehensive. Whatever had frightened her the first time wasn't going to take her by surprise a second time.

Since she slept in the bed that one night a new routine had developed. After spending the evening with us, Winky would ask to go out about 10 P.M. When it was time for bed I put her food in her cage, and we went to bed. Between 5 and 6 A.M. the porch screen door would slam, and in a few moments a raccoon would be in our bed, ready for a little "family togetherness."

That was no hour to tussle with a raccoon, so we just let her stay. She loved it. She would crawl in between us, burrow down under the covers, turn around, and come back up to the head of the bed, where she would sleep with her head on the pillow, partially covered. She thought she was people.

Amusing as it was, deep down I knew we should be working to break her ties with people, not make them more firm. Not that she was a bad bed partner; she was warm and clean and most appreciative, and we didn't mind—until a new dimension was added.

One morning Winky came in early, a little before 5 A.M. She was not yet ready to go to sleep, so she harassed Barbara by playing with her hair, removing her bobby pins, and sticking her finger in Barbara's ear. Thoroughly annoyed, Barbara sat up in bed, picked Winky up, set her down near me, and said, "Now annoy him for a while." Barbara then rolled over and pulled the covers over her head.

Winky sat quietly for a few moments, as if deciding how she could get me to participate in her play. She tentatively patted my head, but there wasn't enough hair there to interest her. I put my hand over my ear, so she couldn't stick her finger in, and for a moment she just lay quietly beside me on the pillow.

A moment or two later, I moved my hand to pat her, saying, "Good girl, now go to sleep." When my hand touched her she grabbed it in both her hands and plopped my thumb in her mouth. In the next instant, she was sucking happily on my thumb and purring.

This thoroughly weaned seven-month-old coon had decided suddenly that she liked to suck thumbs. I retrieved my hand and tried to go back to sleep. Her little hands kept digging under the pillow looking for the thumb I had hidden.

When she found it she grabbed it with both hands and pulled my hand out in the open. Once again she started sucking and purring. At that point I would have let her have the thumb, just to get some sleep, but her purring was so loud I couldn't sleep. I could hear Barbara laughing. I retrieved my thumb once more and rolled over on my stomach with both hands tucked under my abdomen.

With no thumbs available Winky went back over to Barbara, grabbed her hand and began to suck happily. Too tired to fight, Barbara mumbled something about just this once and drifted back to sleep.

After that, we not only had a raccoon in bed with us each morning, but it was a thumb-sucking raccoon at that. And it was our thumb. We kept hoping this was just a passing phase. It was, for our little raccoon was maturing more each day.

On New Year's Eve she decided to celebrate by staying out all night. She left at her usual time, about 10 P.M., but didn't come in at all during the morning. We looked for her all day long when we were outdoors. Was this a repeat of Letta's experience? We both wondered to ourselves, but dared not put it into words.

That evening there was still no sign of a raccoon. About eight-thirty, while we were reading and watching TV, the back door slammed and Winky sauntered into the living room. She couldn't understand what the fuss was all about, but she thoroughly enjoyed all the attention. She stayed with us till bedtime. When I went in to take my shower, she jumped in the shower, too. We were so glad to see her, she would have gotten away with anything that evening.

She stayed in most of the night. About 4 A.M. she wanted to go out. She paced to the door, back to me, patted me gently, and then back to the door. After the third round trip I got the idea and let her out.

For the next week we had a new evening routine. Winky could hear the sounds of the shower from anywhere in the house, and when she heard the water start up she dashed to the bathroom from wherever she was playing and came running.

She hooked her sharp little claws under the edge of the shower door, braced her back feet on the shower-stall curb, leaned back, and hauled the door open. One bound and she was inside, sharing the spray with Barbara or me. She didn't particularly care to shower with the boys, but saved that bit of sharing for us.

While I showered, she sat in the corner enjoying the spray. She took several sips of water flowing down the wall, groomed herself a little, but mostly she just sat blissfully, head down, eyes half-closed, and basked in the warm water.

As I dried myself, she shook a couple of times and joined me on the bath mat. In self-defense I dried her too with her towel, for if I didn't, she ran (coons always seem to run) to the bed, climbed up, and dried herself by rolling on the bedspread.

If I showered first, Winky had a second shower with Barbara. After she was dried, she usually climbed up on the bed and curled up for a nap. If anyone ever told me I would let a raccoon in bed I would have told them they were goofy. But I guess I was the goofy one, because the raccoon was convinced she was people. All week she had been coming to bed with us rather than going out at night like a racoon.

If we went to bed too early for Winky, she played in the bathroom for an hour or so. Her favorite toy was the toilet brush, with which she wrestled and fought. The banging of the toilet brush was our lullaby as we went to sleep. When she was tired enough, she slipped into bed quietly and snuggled up to a warm body.

One night in January started out in the usual way but ended up differently. We were already in bed. Somehow, after Winky had romped with the toilet brush, it appears that she got into the medicine cabinet. She slid the glass door open and investigated each item on the shelf. Among them were drugs for treating the wild creatures brought to me on weekends. Although there were several potentially dangerous preparations, she did not get into these, fortunately. But she did get into some sugar-coated tranquilizing tablets.

She removed the plastic top of the vial, emptied them out on the counter, and had a good time licking the sugar coating off. She swallowed several of the tablets. After that, she didn't come to bed, she staggered to bed. Instead of sleeping quietly, as she usually did, she wiggled about making little "Oooh-whoo" cries and changing position constantly.

Awakened by the movement, I realized that something was wrong. I turned on the light and checked the bathroom. Chaos!

She had wrecked the place! Ointment tubes were chewed, vials opened, lipstick tubes crushed, everything spread from one end of the bathroom to the other. The tranquilizers appeared to be the only thing she had eaten.

A bleary-eyed coon peered at me from the bed as I explained to Barbara what happened. The tranquilizers were rather mild, and the amount she had taken should not have been a fatal dose. However, instead of quieting her down they were "hopping" her up.

As I turned off the light and went back to bed, hoping for some sleep, the situation worsened. Winky suddenly became a rowdy drunk. She grabbed fingers and tried to suck them, she cried, she wiggled, she made other weird little noises, she paced back and forth over the pillows—there was no quieting her.

I couldn't put her outside in this condition, no telling what might happen to her. So I put her on the screened porch. She cried, and began pulling everything down as she staggered about. Finally we wrapped her in a towel and brought her back to bed. She rested fitfully until the first light of morning when we all got up. Our little drunk paced through the house all morning. She followed us outdoors, and then followed us back.

A bleary-eyed little coon dogged our footsteps all day long. With no sleep her disposition was terrible. She growled and hissed at everything, but she couldn't stand to be away from us.

Barbara tried to soothe her by giving her a bottle but Winky only bit off the end of the nipple and swallowed it, spilling milk everywhere.

In the evening, finally, she began to slow down. The drugs were wearing off. She curled up in front of the fireplace and slept in the fire's warmth.

After she had had her two showers she, too, was ready to go to bed. Three weary creatures crawled into bed that night and slept well.

In the morning John summed it up: "That was a real bad trip Winky had!" he said.

It didn't seem possible, but a whole year had gone by since Winky had come to live with us. During the past several months there were several more changes in her habits. She spent more of the nights outdoors, and came in about 6 A.M.

Instead of sleeping with us, she usually climbed up on the top shelf of the bedroom closet and slept there for the whole day. She was still sweet and gentle with us, but she didn't like to be picked up. In the evening she would come and sit in my lap. She liked to be petted and scratched, but she was past the age when she would allow herself to be cuddled.

She was getting very protective about the house. If we had visitors or guests, and she heard strange sounds and voices, she would slip into the living room, creep under a chair, and bite whatever leg she could reach.

After the second person had been bitten, we kept her locked away from guests, for she just wasn't to be trusted. We knew for certain we had made a grievous error in judgment in allowing her to become so dependent upon us. We shouldn't have let her sleep with us, but should have insisted that she sleep outdoors. If we had, she would have been ready to cut her bonds with humans. We could have provided security, food, and love during the day, but should have forced her to spend more time learning to be a raccoon.

Now it was going to be twice as hard on her and on us to break the habits that bound her to us. A time came when she had bitten four people. We had to do something at once.

Since we were due to be leaving on vacation that seemed like the best time to make her stay out. Food would be provided for her while we were gone, and John and I would build several houses she could use outdoors.

We started two nights before we left. After she went out at eleven, we locked the screen door to the porch, so she couldn't come back in. She busied herself all night and as usual came back at dawn to let herself in. I heard the door "snap" as she pulled the bottom of the screen door to open it. I got out of bed and peeked out on the porch to watch her.

She hooked her little hands under the door and began to yank. The bottom of the flexible screen door opened about an inch and slammed shut. Winky sat down on the step, looked up at the door handle, stood up on her hind legs, and reached for the door handle. She had to climb up on the screen to reach it, but then she held onto the handle with both hands, braced her feet against the door jamb, and pulled and tugged. The handle wouldn't budge.

When she could hang on no longer she dropped down, made a feeble pull at the bottom of the door, gave a little churring, piteous "Oooh-whoo" cry, and walked down and around the corner of the house without as much as touching her food.

As she walked past our window she gave two more soft, piteous cries—as if asking, "How can you do this to me?" then continued on into the woods.

It was all I could do to keep from calling her back and

Winky comes to the roof feeder at night.

unlocking the door. Any sound from me and she would have come running back. I forced myself to be silent, but as I crawled back into bed I couldn't force myself back to sleep. I just lay looking at the ceiling and feeling bad.

The next evening when she came back we let her in to visit with us. When it came time for her to go out at eleven, she didn't want to go. She knew that if she went out, she might not get back in. Feeling like a traitor, I coaxed her outside with a few peanuts and a couple of minimarshmallows.

After she left, I locked the door. I hoped I would not

hear her when she returned in the morning, but I heard her before she even tried the door, and I could anticipate each move and sound she would make. It was a repeat of the previous morning, and I found it even more difficult to resist her calls for assistance. I did not relent, however. After she left I put on my clothes and slipped out the door and into the woods.

I had seen the direction she had taken when she left the house, so as quietly as possible I followed, scanning each tree carefully as I moved along. A hundred yards from the house I saw her. Perched in the crotch of a big oak tree about thirty feet off the ground, she lay looking at me. She glared and hissed at me. I pretended not to see her, I did not speak, but turned and angled off into the woods and away from her perch. Then I circled around and returned to the house.

I was relieved. At least I knew where she was sleeping during the day. We would see that fresh water and food were put out for her each day while we were gone.

In our absence, my parents and Bruce Thomas, a sixteen-year-old neighbor boy, saw to it that all the animals were fed and cared for, including Winky.

After our fourth day away from home we called to see if everything was all right. They hadn't actually seen Winky, but her food was disappearing each evening, so she was eating.

Ten days later we called again. My mother had spent the night at our house, and she had seen Winky. Winky had come in the morning and had tried the screen door. When it would not open for her, she went around to the front of the house and tried to force the windows open.

She wanted to get into her house.

When four days later we arrived home at about nine in the evening, just as the last light of day was fading, the dogs came to greet us, and Pirtle, the Gambel quail, started calling from the porch when he heard our voices. As I went around to the back door I heard another calling. The trembling, quavering call of a lost raccoon. It was Winky using her "I'm lost" call, one she hadn't given since she was four months old. I looked, but couldn't see her. I heard her again. As I followed the sound I found one of the unused nest boxes barricaded against the porch wall near the door. She was inside, but why had she been barricaded in?

I turned the box around to free her, she peeked out at me, called again, and then hissed at me. She wanted me to help her, but she wanted me to stay away. She was a mixed-up lady.

As I backed away from the box, she jumped out, purring and churring as she went to Barbara and then tried the screen door. It opened for her. She ran a little way on the porch and then came back outside again. She went back inside the nest box and came out carrying a baby raccoon. We all just stood there dumbfounded. Winky wasn't waiting for congratulations.

She dropped the baby, quickly opened the screen door, then grabbed up the baby again and trotted across the porch, through the living room, down the hall, and into John's room. There, she climbed the louvered doors of his closet and deposited the baby on the top shelf.

Then she raced down and back outside and repeated the whole procedure with another baby. After she left I reached into the nest box. It was empty. She had had two babies while we were gone. Finally she managed to get them into "her" house where she felt they belonged.

I had to call my parents and find out the story behind the barricade. When my father answered, he told me in no uncertain terms that the coon had to go. It had bitten Bruce's mother and my mother when they had approached the nest box. They had no idea she had babies in the box. What they had interpreted as a vicious, unprovoked attack was a confused mother trying to protect her babies from strangers. Neither of the ladies had been seriously bitten, but both had suffered sore, painful bites. I apologized to my mother and to Bruce's mother. I promised both we would try to get her to be a wild coon again as soon as possible.

But how was I going to do that? Winky had finally got into her house after three weeks of trying and she wasn't leaving again.

For the next two days she left those babies only long enough to go into the bathroom and use the toilet. Then she would race back to John's room and climb back onto the shelf. Barbara kept food on the lower shelf for her.

On the third day she moved the babies into our room, to the top shelf of Barbara's closet. She did her moving at about three in the morning. This made her new home more convenient to the bathroom, and I guess she could look down from her tower and keep track of us.

The next night she was much more active. She still wouldn't come near me, but she had made up with Barbara, since Barbara was there all day. Each time I came near her after I came home from work she would growl and hiss—so I just stayed away.

The second night when I was taking my shower she

couldn't resist. I heard her climbing down the closet door as I turned on the water. I went in and closed the door to prevent any encounter, but she was ready for her shower.

She pulled open the door and danced in under the water. Then she seemed to realize that I was there with her. She growled and grabbed my heel in her teeth. She didn't bite down. I stood still, but I spoke loudly and sharply to her, telling her to behave. She turned my heel loose and went to her corner where she usually basked in the warm water and enjoyed the rest of her shower.

After her shower she was beginning to be a little more relaxed—and not quite as fearful, but she would still be dangerous if she were crowded or pushed.

I would have to find some way to get her outside, so she could have more freedom and the babies would grow up more normally. I fell asleep pondering how I could do it with the least harm to her nervous system.

In the early hours of the morning I awoke. Lying still I listened, not sure what had caused me to wake up. Then I felt it. A tug of the blanket as Winky pulled herself up on the bed. I felt her walk alongside me, touching me gently as she moved. I felt her cold nose as she sniffed my back and neck. I lay perfectly still as she buried her nose in my hair and patted my ear as she walked across the pillow toward Barbara.

I didn't know if she were on the way to bite me or not. But as she began to play with Barbara's hair, as she had when she was a baby, I knew everything was all right and she had relaxed.

When she stuck her finger into Barbara's ear, Barbara sat up with a quick, sudden jolt that scared both Winky and me.

Winky fled to the bathroom while I reassured Barbara that the monsters weren't after her.

As we both settled down, Winky was playing in the bathtub and I still had my problem to ponder—how do you move a raccoon family out of "their" house?

Sometimes in the night, during deepest sleep, the answers come, and in the morning when I woke up I knew what must be done.

I would bring in the big box trap, a large box with a treadle in the floor. The door automatically closed when anything stepped on it. It doesn't hurt a prisoner, but any animal caught in this way can be handled without danger to itself. I would bait the trap with marshmallows, after-dinner mints, and peanuts—Winky's favorite foods. When she entered to eat, she would step on the treadle and trap herself. We could then move her and the trap to the roof.

I told John and Barbara of the plan. They agreed. Tonight was the night.

John and I constructed a large dry house of cypress two-by-sixes on the flat porch roof. John was to take the babies and put them in the house. I would carry Winky up in the trap and release her into the house where the babies waited for her. While she was checking her babies, John and I would make our escape down the ladder.

But even the best-laid plans don't always work out. At dusk a gentle rain started to fall, and by dark it was pouring. The plan was scrapped for the night. I think we were all relieved that we didn't have to be "ogres" and kick our baby out into the night.

The next morning Winky was sweet to everyone, but by evening she was her protective self. She ran John out of his bedroom once, growling, snarling, and acting as if she would eat him alive. He moved too quickly for her, but after he almost got caught and cornered, he voted to carry out our plan that night, rain or clear.

Since Winky's first stop was always the bathroom when she got up in the evening, I placed the trap in the bathroom door. She would have to go into the trap to go to the bathroom.

Around ten, I heard her climbing down from the closet shelf. She rummaged around in the bottom of the closet for a moment and headed for the bathroom. She sniffed the entrance of the trap thoroughly and then nonchalantly walked away and headed down the hall to John's bathroom. The first part of the plan hadn't worked. I put some peanuts in the trap. Maybe the smell of peanuts would get her.

We went back to the living room to leave her undisturbed. At ten-thirty the door of the trap slammed shut. I jumped up and ran into the bedroom expecting to see a trapped raccoon. I knew it wouldn't take long for her to figure out the combination necessary to get the door open and get out. The trap was empty, and Winky was leering at me from the closet shelf.

Mumbling a couple of bad words under my breath, I said, "Winky, we just can't have you terrorizing family and friends, now please be a good girl and let us catch you. We love you, but you have to raise those kids outdoors."

I didn't make any impression on her; she just hissed gently at me as I came over to talk to her. As I looked up at her, I tried to find some excuse to let her stay, but I knew it was best for her, and for us, if she raised those babies outside where they would learn to be normal raccoons and not emotional cripples dependent upon people.

I reset the trap and set it in the opening of the folding closet doors. I closed the doors against the sides of the trap and tied them in position with a thong around the two door handles, then I put two boxes of books on top of the trap. "Now, if you want to leave the closet, you are going to have to go into the trap, Winky. Besides, look at the goodies in there, and we've got a nice house ready for you. Be a good girl and cooperate."

No such luck. We went to bed with the raccoon looking at us from the shelf. She appeared to be ready to spend the next week on the shelf rather than give in to my unreasonable demands.

As soon as I fell asleep I was banged awake by the slamming of the trap door. I jumped up, turned on the light, and checked the trap. No raccoon. She had sprung it again and hadn't trapped herself. Now that she knew how it worked we couldn't catch her that way.

She growled at me from the bottom of the closet as I moved the trap out of the way. She climbed to her shelf as I started back to bed. Like two contenders, we looked at each other, each plotting a next move. I didn't have a good plan, so I turned off the light and decided to sleep on the problem again. Maybe the answer would come as I slept, as it did before.

Sleep didn't come, for while I didn't have any plans, Winky had hers. Every few minutes she pushed something else off one of the closet shelves. She was doing it deliberately. She had been coming and going on those shelves for six days without knocking anything off. Now every few minutes something was being pulled out and dropped to the floor.

I stood it for as long as I could, then got up and turned on the light. I called John in. And under the glare of our problem coon, we had another council.

We all agreed we couldn't go on this way. We all needed more sleep at night. Winky was the problem and the sooner it was solved the freer we would all be.

Barbara got an old blanket, John got the stepladder, and I put on my clothes and a pair of gloves. There was no easy way. I would have to climb up and wrap her in the blanket to confine her and to keep from being bitten, and we would forcibly move her right then.

With the blanket held in front of me as a protective barrier, I climbed the stepladder to the closet shelf. Only someone who has faced an angry raccoon eye to eye can appreciate what this means. A whirlwind of teeth and claws hurled itself at me as she growled, spit, and jumped, snapping her teeth and biting the blanket.

Our sweet, playful friend of a few months ago wasn't there anymore. This ferocious mother meant to protect her babies. I tried to talk softly and move slowly, but as I tried to envelop her in the blanket it turned into a wild free-for-all.

Everything on the closet shelves began sailing through the air as Winky squirmed around biting and trying to avoid being caught. Sometimes she was in the lead, sometimes I was. After what seemed like an age, but was actually only a short time, I had her entangled and rolled up in the blanket.

I called to John to get the babies and I ran outside. John and I climbed the ladder to the roof. He put the babies in the new house, placed a dish of food on the floor, and I tried to release Winky inside.

Instead, her head suddenly popped out of a fold against my abdomen. I knew she had me, but in the couple of seconds that she took to look about, I quickly set her and the blanket down at the entrance of her house.

She stuck her head in, grabbed one of her kits, and dragged it out. She watched me, but didn't growl. She appeared very subdued. I felt that if I could get away, she might settle down and take the baby back inside the house.

My route of escape, the ladder, was near her. I was afraid she would run away and desert her baby if I approached her. Instead, I went to the far side of the roof and climbed down the TV antenna. We went inside and turned off the lights, hoping that with everything quiet she would feel safe. We even left the mess all over the bedroom floor. With whispered comments on the whole affair we each tried to go to sleep.

It was a fitful sleep at best. My conscience hurt, and I felt I had let her down some way. My hope was that everything would work out right in the end.

First thing in the morning I climbed up on the roof quietly. Winky was not in the house. She was gone—everything was gone. Then I thought I heard something inside.

I reached through the entrance and, groping blindly, touched something warm. I brought the "something" out and there was the smaller of Winky's two babies. Winky had left. But she had left a baby behind. Had she deserted it?

All day long the question nagged at us. Barbara wanted to bring the baby down and feed it, but I talked her out of it.

Her mother had only been gone twelve hours. If she came back that night, the baby would have been by itself fewer than twenty-four hours, which would not harm it. If it were still there in the morning, we would bring it in and start feeding it then.

That night I put fresh dog food in Winky's bowl, garnished it with a few raisins and a couple of minimarshmallows, and placed it near the house on the roof.

I listened for her, but heard nothing. First thing in the morning I climbed the ladder to the roof. I hoped that during the night she would have brought her other baby back and that all three of them would live happily ever after in the home we had built for them. Instead the house was completely empty. She had been back, taken the baby, and returned to the woods.

The food we had put in her house hadn't been touched. She was "pouting." Whenever she got angry at us she would refuse to eat, and this was the angriest she had ever been.

We had the relief of knowing she had both of her babies. A new concern was that she was not eating. It seemed as if we leaped from problem to problem with this little raccoon in the thirteen months we had her.

In the evening I put fresh food in the house with its

garnish of peanuts and raisins. All evening we listened for her. She would be quite hungry now and would be coming early for food if we were forgiven.

At ten I heard a pebble fall from the roof. I took a flashlight and Barbara and I went out and played the beam around the house on the roof. There she was. Our little masked baby girl was peeking cautiously around the corner at us.

Barbara spoke to her, "We're sorry, Winky. We'll feed you and pet you when you let us, but you can't bring the babies in." Cocking her head sideways as if she were listening to every word, she stared at Barbara as she talked to her. Then she came to the edge of the roof and looked down at us. As Barbara talked to her softly with all the words all mothers speak to their babies, Winky climbed down the big owl cage that joined the porch roof.

First she let Barbara pet her, but she wouldn't have anything to do with me. I was the man who had tossed her out. Next thing I knew she had climbed on Barbara's shoulder. No fierceness, no biting, just the old Winky we used to know.

Since she was made to feel welcome, I guess she figured all was forgiven again, for she climbed down Barbara's arm and headed for the door.

I had visions of her getting back to the security of her closet shelf and choosing to stay with her human friends at the expense of the tiny raccoon babies. As she started to open the door I reached my arm over her and held the door closed. "Winky, we can't let you in, baby. You have to take care of those babies." She looked up, spit at me like

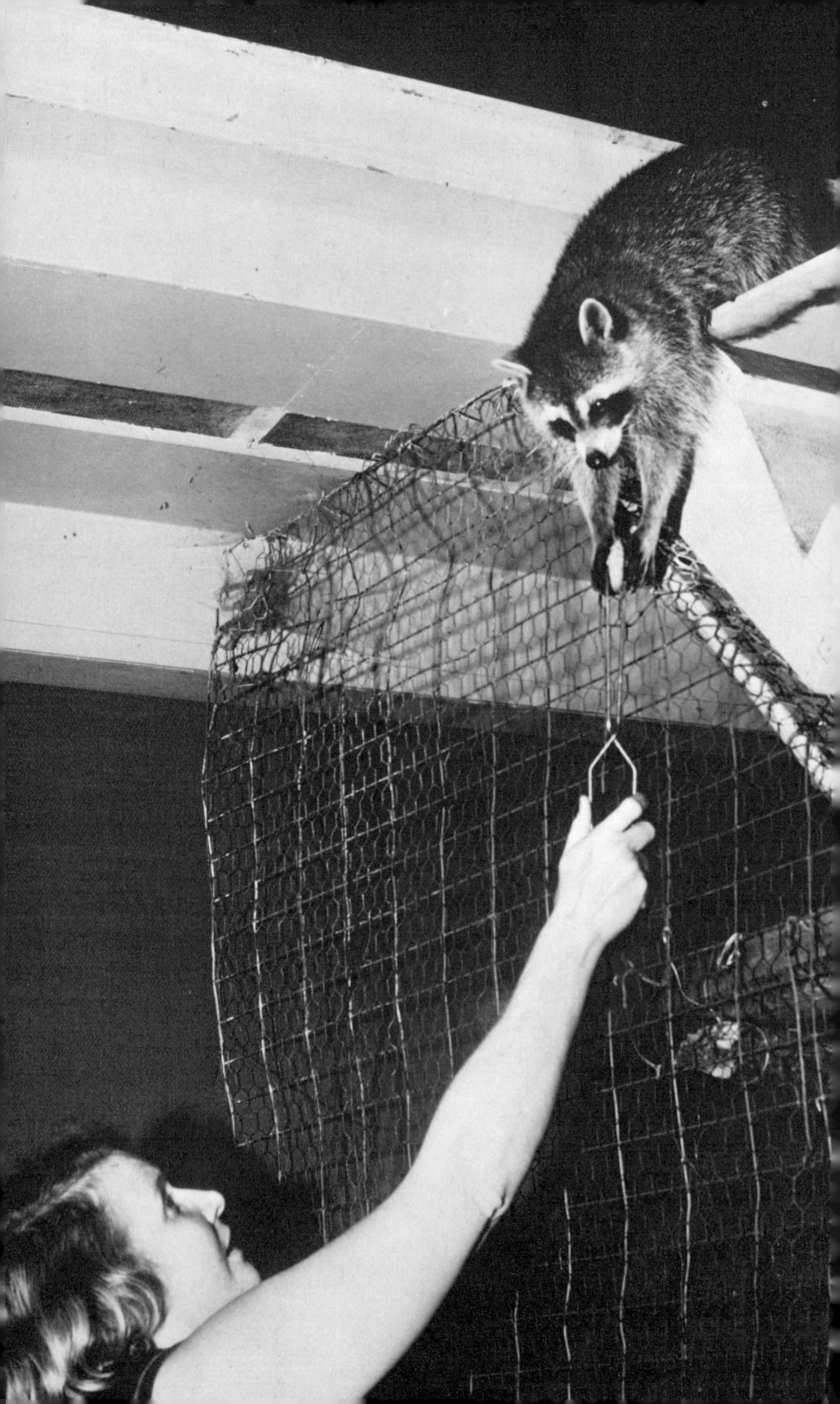

an angry cat, and then climbed the big cage to the roof.

Animals do have expressions that show emotion, and this little raccoon definitely looked betrayed.

She hissed and spit at both of us as she reached the roof, so I knew I was interpreting her correctly. She didn't look at us again as she trudged off across the roof into the darkness.

She didn't eat for two more days. I tried to tempt her, but to no avail. She left pebbles in the water I put out for her, so I knew she had been there in the night, but she didn't touch the food.

Finally, hunger won out. She began to eat. The next few nights, she ate twice as much as usual. We had reached an uneasy peace. She would accept the food I provided, she would raise her babies as we desired, but no more friendship.

During the next month, the few times that any of us saw her late in the evening, she would hiss and growl as she retreated into the darkness. Perhaps she had become a normal wild mother after all. Certainly her babies would be raised to be wary, wild creatures, and that was important. Food would be provided as long as she desired it, for the obligation we owed her was important. We raised her to expect help from people, and we would never let her down.

Winky forgives us and accepts a cookie from Barbara.

:5:
Bob,
a Bobwhite Quail

Lisa and her sister Marva got off their bicylces and came to the back porch. Lisa opened her cupped hand to show me the little bird she had found and asked if I would help.

The little bird was only as big as a marble and covered with soft buff down. Its head was the size of a pea. A shiny brown eye calmly looked up at me. As I took the tiny creature, Lisa told me she had found it in their back yard. It had fallen from its nest in the big oak tree.

I explained that it was a quail chick, and instead of falling from the tree, it had probably gotten lost from its mother as it followed her through their yard. My observation seemed to satisfy the two little girls. Reassured that I knew something about birds, they expressed their thanks and left the little orphan with us.

The little quail was content to sit in my hand and watch the preparations the boys made for its welfare. When the nest was complete, I placed the chick where it could rest and get warm.

It was bright and alert, but would not eat any seeds or

mash regardless how it was offered. The little chick seemed unafraid. Yet, no matter how I tempted it, it would not eat. I suggested to the boys that we allow it to rest in the warmth of its nest and try again in the morning.

The next morning the baby still refused to eat. When we took it from the nest, it was unafraid and alert. It walked about calmly in the area where we had spread bits of chick starter mash and parakeet seed, but did not eat. It was almost unreal to see this tiny bit of fluff no bigger than a thumbnail walk about, cock its head, and peer up at you with its tiny brown eyes.

I began to get worried. The tiny creature could not live without food. In desperation, I dipped a toothpick in some of the regular formula and touched the drop of liquid to the tiny quail's beak. Some of the liquid entered its mouth and it swallowed. It looked expectantly up at me, seeming to want more. As I offered more, it reached for each drop that was presented. The boys and I congratulated ourselves. We had found a way to get food into the baby. It should live.

After a day of eating formula, the little chick began to try the other foods, too. Soon, with the same cocky self-confidence it was to show all the rest of its life, the little quail came expectantly to meet us each time we approached the nest. It hopped eagerly to our hands to see what new treasure we were bringing.

A month later the baby grew enough feathers to tell us he was a male bird. He was no longer content to stay in a cage. He wanted to be where the people were. Everyone had to walk carefully to keep from stepping on this little tan butterfly that fluttered around underfoot.

In a couple of weeks he began flying, testing his wings

Baby quail picks a drop of formula off end of toothpick.

on short flights around the porch. Now he was no longer underfoot, but on someone's shoulder or head. He was always on the table at mealtime.

The boys had read *That Quail, Robert*, so this quail, since it was a male and a bobwhite quail, was called Bob. He adopted John as his parent and protector.

He followed John everywhere. When John went outside, the little quail trailed along behind him. If John went too

Bob

fast for him, little Bob would stop, crouch down dejectedly, and give a plaintive, whistling call, which in quail language seemed to say, "I am lost, I am lost." John would have to go back, pick him up, place him on his shoulder, and then they would go on.

If John had to leave the yard, he would put Bob back in on the porch. The little quail would not let up his protests. He repeated "I am lost, I am lost" over and over. He refused to be consoled by any of us. After a while he would give up. He would stop calling and begin to sulk.

When John came home, the little quail would sing out his "I am lost" call as soon as he heard John's voice. He would leave the nest, run to him, and whistle and peep rudely to let John know how angry he had been.

He slept with John at night, snuggling up to him on the pillow as close as he could get. In the morning, he was ready to get up at sunrise. He expected John to get up, too. If John wanted to sleep later, he had to cover his head with the covers to fend off the harassing pecks of the now almost mature quail.

Like a dignified young man, he walked beside John to the breakfast table and had his share of John's milk and cereal. On school days, as soon as John left, Bob would go out on the porch, bask in the sun on the porch rail, and talk to the other quail and birds that came to the feeder in the back yard.

He was grown now. He would give the bobwhite call of the adult quail, and always answer when other quail called. He could leave by the porthole in the porch screen, which he sometimes did, to join the other quail searching for birdseed under the feeder in the back yard. But when they left, he always returned to the porch.

In the evenings he was ready to go to bed when the sun went down, but he patiently waited for John to go to bed. He would nap in an empty ashtray on the table beside my chair, or go down to the floor where he would curl up next to one of the sleeping dogs. He would push up against one of the dachshunds, find a little nook he could fit into, and nap contentedly in the radiant warmth of their bodies.

Bob seemed to regard himself as a human, and never recognized himself as a bird. He joined us at every meal, and while he usually had impeccable table manners, there were times when he left something to be desired.

One suppertime, Bob, as usual, went around the table checking out everyone's plate to see whose was the most appetizing and who would have the honor of sharing supper with him. I was selected. With his shiny beak, he speared a green pea from my plate and placed it on the table, near my coffee cup. He leisurely picked the skin off the tiny vegetable and ate the insides.

Having finished the pea, he started back for more. He placed one foot on the edge of the plate and reached across it, past a dozen or so peas, for the most distant pea on the plate. With one foot on the plate and the other on the table, his footing was precarious, and he slipped. He would have fallen breast first into the chicken gravy, but I reached out quickly and scooped him up in my hand, saving both him and my supper.

His feet falling between my fingers, he pedaled frantically as if trying to regain his footing on the smooth surfaces of the plate and table. When he seemed to have settled, I set him down and turned him loose. He skated unsteadily toward the bowl of applesauce, made a little leap, and landed on the rim of the bowl. Still treading for secure footing he slipped, caught himself, teetered, slipped again, and fell backward into my glass of milk. As Bob flapped his wings to right and lift himself out of the glass, a shower of milk sprinkled everyone at the table.

I helped him out of the milk. A thoroughly disgruntled bird stood beside the glass. He looked disgustedly at all

Bob checks out John's plate.

the faces laughing at him, shook the remaining milk from his feathers, and walked pompously to the edge of the table. With a backward glance of reproach, he flew to the floor.

He turned his back on us and snuggled up to Julia, the dachshund. As I watched him he opened an eye to see if we were still looking at him. When he saw that I was still watching him, he turned his back on me, as if to ignore us completely.

After several minutes hunger overcame his indignation, and he returned to the table and finished his supper.

On only one other occasion did Bob have a tabletop accident. That time, he did fall into the gravy. While it was funny when it happened, it turned out to be serious. I was not home at the time.

He was hurrying as he foraged around the table, and he slipped. To catch his balance, he fluttered his wings and lifted a few inches off the table. This height and the forward momentum carried him to the edge of the gravy dish. While his feet gripped the edge of the bowl securely, he had too much forward momentum to stop altogether, and he tipped forward like a falling tree, landing face first in the warm gravy. A bedraggled, oily, matted lump emerged. The boys laughed at him as they reached for him to clean him off.

It was almost instantly apparent that Bob was in trouble. His mouth was open. He gasped for air, and staggered as he tried to walk. Bill picked him up and wrapped him quickly in a towel. Holding his head downward, he half-shook and half-swung Bob to force the gravy from his nostrils and throat. When he tipped him back up, the greasy little bird could breathe, but he still looked sick as he gazed up at Bill from half-closed lids.

The boys placed him on the floor to see if he could walk. He took a few steps, staggered, and fell sideways. Bill assumed that with his balance affected, his ears were involved, so when he picked him up, he parted the greasy feathers over the ear openings and checked. The right opening was full of gravy. With bits of cotton, he wiped gently at the gooey mess around the ear. The bird shook his head, helping to dislodge the rest of the gravy from the ear canal.

Now Bob could walk and breathe normally. But the feathers, clotted together as they were, had lost their insulating value. He just shook and shivered. Barbara, Bill, and John cleaned and absorbed the oil with facial tissue. Even when the tissue supply was exhausted, Bob still remained a slimy mess.

Barbara finally decided on a radical course of action. While Bill and John held and steadied the bird, she had them immerse him up to his neck in warm dishwater. Surprisingly, Bob didn't struggle. Perhaps it was the warmth of the water that soothed him or perhaps he no longer cared. But he remained still in the boys' hands while their mother fluffed his feathers back and forth in the soapy water.

When all the stickiness was gone and the feathers seemed to float freely, they rinsed him in warm water from the tap. While Bill cradled him in a warm bath towel, Barbara set up her hair dryer on the couch. One boy on each side of him for moral support, Bob stood on a towel in front of the warm air from the dryer.

Gradually the feathers began to dry and Bob began to

come back. Starting with a feeble little shake, he rearranged his feathers. As the feathers dried and assumed a feather shape, Bob preened and shook them out more vigorously.

In thirty minutes the crisis was over. Bob, new and shiny from his bath, fluttered down off the couch, stalked into the kitchen, and moved in beside Julia at her feeding dish. He helped himself to a couple of beakfuls of her dog food. Surprised at his audacity, Julia just looked at him. The rest of the family relaxed, knowing that Bob was all right and back to his normal cocky self again.

Bob was a self-appointed guardian of the house. He didn't like strangers, and in particular, he didn't like children or ladies in open-toed shoes. In his old age he would intimidate young children by pecking at them, and if this didn't work he would fly at them. Even the bravest youngster fled when this mass of brown, whirling feather descended on his head.

Lady guests in sandals or open-toed shoes were more vulnerable. He would peck at their toes. They didn't want to offend us by kicking out at the little bird, but the pecking did hurt.

We finally had to banish Bob to the aviary when guests came. He enjoyed some of our friends. James Gregg liked sugar and lemon in his tea and was willing to share it with Bob. Carroll Gregg always greeted Bob by picking him up and cuddling him for a moment or two before she carefully placed him on the floor. Bob would ruffle his feathers up and stalk off indignantly, but I am sure he liked the attention.

There were a few others of our friends he would tolerate, but in general he became a rather crotchety old man.

:6:
Squirrels, Squirrels, Squirrels

Chortles was a baby gray squirrel and appeared to be about two weeks old. The first time I saw her, she was as big as a mouse. She was pink all over, and her eyes were still sealed shut. Genie Wilson, a good friend, brought her into the office. During a windstorm the previous night, the baby squirrel had fallen from a nest in the big hickory tree in her back yard.

Genie found it early in the morning. She warmed the baby in her hands, but left it at the base of the tree. She hoped the mother would come down and retrieve her baby. When the baby was still there late in the morning, she brought it in.

I took the tiny thing home to raise. Gray squirrel babies are fun to raise, because they are hardy and have the ability to survive with even minimum care. They adapt well to people and adapt well to freedom when it is offered. They are alert, lively creatures, and each has a different personality. It is always fun to see how each is going to turn out.

This baby enjoyed the companionship of people at once. She liked to crawl up into a hand whenever she heard or felt a person near her nest box. Finally, she grew a little hair, and her black, beady eyes opened.

At this age, whenever she saw one of us coming to her nest box, she would immediately get up, come to the edge of the nest, place her little front feet on the edge of the box, and lean out. All the while she made a little trilling sound of greeting. It was a soft, happy noise, which we came to call "chortling," and she naturally came to be called Chortles.

When we were close enough she leaped to us, clinging with her sharp little claws. Then she crawled up to your shoulder and snuggled up under your chin, still making her little chortling, greeting sound.

Even when she was almost grown, she still liked to crawl under a sweater or shirt and snuggle up to a warm body. In the evenings she would find a warm spot somewhere against one of us, and she would sleep while we sat and read or watched TV.

Many gray squirrels get nippy, wild, and aggressive when they begin to mature. Some are selfish and greedy; others, shy and gentle. Chortles was shy and gentle. We have always been partial to the shy, gentle ones, because they seem to need us most.

As Chortles grew up she went outside four or five times a day and played for short intervals, but she spent most of her time in the house. At night she always slept in her nest house on the porch.

In the morning she came to breakfast with the family. She helped herself from everyone's plate and had milk,

Chortles, a friendly gray squirrel

cereal, and toast with us. She regarded herself as part of the family. During the day she helped with the housekeeping riding on Barbara's shoulder or in her apron pocket. She supervised the entire operation of the house.

When things were quiet during the day, she occupied herself by building little nests in various parts of the house. Her favorite place was behind the draperies. She would steal a Kleenex from the box in the kitchen, roll it up into a little ball, and then carry it in her teeth to the nest site. Here she would unroll it and tuck it in between the drapery rods and the wall. After numerous such trips she had a soft little nest made to her satisfaction. She would use it as a napping place for a day or so and then start another nest, in a new site.

She spent some time each day setting up her little food hoards. Nuts were hidden in the bookcase, kernels were removed from the ears of corn in our cornucopia and hidden behind the music stand of the piano, acorns were hidden in shoes in the closets. Like a little miser, she checked each item in her hoard daily.

She was so much a part of the family, we just accepted her sleeping on top of the draperies or curled up in a corner of the armchair. She followed Barbara everywhere, inside the house and out. Then one day it happened. As she followed Barbara indoors, she didn't move through the door with her usual speed and agility. The heavy door closed on her, snuffing out this gentle spirit in an instant. It was then that we realized how much a part of the family she had become; how much we missed this furry little pixie.

Of all the gray squirrels we raised, only some were

Chortles between the drapery rods and the wall.

given names. There were Rascal, Rommel, Twiggy, and the Twins. Many never got names. Of them all, there is one other squirrel that stands out in our memory.

Snowflake, too, was tiny and pink when we got her, but her eyes were open and she had soft white fur covering most of her body. Snowflake was an albino gray squirrel. Her red eyes had a friendly twinkle, and her pink paws were gentle as they grasped you when you came near her nest box.

She was never as dependent upon people as Chortles had been, but she was always glad to see us. When she got older, she spent most of the daytime hours outside, frisking through the treetops like a little white streak.

Snowflake

When she heard any of us outside she literally flew to us, landing on a shoulder as she jumped the last distance to reach us. Most squirrels become wary and more nearly wild outdoors, but Flaky, as we ended up calling her, was always friendly.

She would rest on a shoulder as we went about our chores outdoors, or crawl into a jacket pocket—hoping to find a nut that had been forgotten there. As long as we had her she never got angry or ever tried to bite a human friend.

While her days were spent outdoors, she came in on the porch several times each day to get a snack from the store of nuts she kept cached in her cage on the porch. Sometimes she brought a friend in with her. Ladylike, she would bring her friend to her cage, climb in to show her about, and then share a nut with her young gray companion.

Even when mature, Snowflake returned each day at dusk to the porch. She visited with each of us for a few moments, and then, as if assured that her family was well, she retired to her nest home for the night. She was an early riser and was always gone in the morning by the time we got up. Later in the morning she would visit with Barbara as she hung up the wash or went outside on some other errand.

In the late autumn she started spending some nights away from home. She had found her own niche in the squirrel world in the woods around the house. As she became more secure in her new world she spent fewer and fewer nights at home. Finally she stopped coming altogether.

We knew her beautiful white coat made her much more visible and vulnerable to such predators as hawks and owls as she moved through the trees; but we could not confine her, even for her own sake. We like to think that she found a territory of her own and is still living happily. But it has been a long time since we have seen a white squirrel anywhere in the woods.

In our area we have three types of squirrels. The gray

squirrel, the most common, the southern flying squirrel, and the large fox squirrel. We seldom see the fox squirrels and have never raised a baby one.

The flying squirrels are nocturnal creatures, and are much smaller and shier than the gray squirrels. Most people don't realize how common and prevalent they are, because they are seldom seen. When full-grown, they are not much larger than a big mouse. They have soft silken fur and large black eyes. When we got Princess, she was about as big around as my thumb and a little over an inch long. Even as a tiny baby she was quick to learn and mastered taking formula from the medicine dropper at once.

Because she was so cute and dainty even as a baby, she received a great deal of attention and cuddling. By the time her eyes were open and she had her first fur coat, she liked to spend the evenings with us. She seemed to enjoy crawling into a shirt pocket, curling up in a little ball, and sleeping next to the warmth of a body. This was the start of her day, and she wasn't an early starter.

When she got a little older and more active, she was given the freedom of the whole house in the evening and at night. The cats were put outside, and Princess's cage door was opened. Since flying squirrels are night creatures, this is the time of day she wanted to play. She romped across the chairs, up the draperies, sailed off into space to land with a soft "plop" on the carpet. Then she would run to one of us, waiting to be congratulated on her beautiful jump. She would stop for a snack of nuts and bits of fruit from the little bowl placed on the table for her. If she found a particularly delicious morsel she would carry it up inside my sweater sleeve, or down inside my shirt, or someone else's, to eat it in the warm, dark security such spots offered her.

The boys found it impossible to sit still under the tickling sensation her wiggling caused as she maneuvered into a position that finally suited her. Often when she finished her snack, she would take a short nap right there in the same spot before coming out to play again. After several weeks of this behavior we became accustomed to sitting in a way so as not to squash the little warm lump in our sleeve.

Her favorite playground was the boys' room. She went with them when they went to bed. When the lights went off it was Princess's fun time. She climbed the closet doors and venetian blinds and sailed off the top of each to land on one bed or the other. She romped with John's stuffed animals in the closet and then visited each boy in turn several times before they fell asleep. She slipped under the covers with them, investigated toes, fingers, pajama buttons, and all the other things that stimulated the little flying squirrel's curiosity. Giggles from the darkness of the room was evidence that they enjoyed this activity as much as she did.

The boys put a few nuts and bits of fruit in a shallow dish on their chest of drawers for her nighttime eating pleasure. She ate and played long after they fell asleep.

Occasionally she would visit our room during the night, too. We got used to the little furry whiskers and the tiny paws that touched our ear in the darkness and even to the tiny body that snuggled up to our neck or arm for a nap during the night.

In the morning Princess was placed in her cage and nest house on the porch. This was for her security. With four cats coming and going in the house it wouldn't do for her to decide to take a daylight stroll. But before we could move her outside, we had to find her first.

She was usually in one of two places—asleep in some little cave among the stuffed animals on John's closet shelf, or sleeping in his pajama drawer, between the flannel pajamas. When she was found the routine was always the same.

She hated to be disturbed. When she was uncovered, she would stand up to her full three-inch height and chirp out her displeasure at being awakened. As soon as we picked her up, however, she would snuggle down into our hands and allow herself to be carried out to the porch.

She was truly a dainty, regal little princess and not at all like Ace, the flying squirrel that came along several years later. Big, fat, bumbling old Ace still lives with us.

Ace was never really a gentle, friendly little flying squirrel. He was an independent spirit. When he was grown he adopted a nest house in the aviary.

Frequently other flying squirrels which come along are placed in the aviary, too. When they are grown or healed, we open the small trap door at the top so our guests can leave whenever they wish, or they can come and go as they please until they adapt to freedom. After a time, when they no longer use the aviary facilities, the trap door is closed. Eventually, they all choose freedom. That is, all except Ace.

He has had numerous opportunities to leave. Even when we tore down the screen walls of the aviary and

Ace, flying squirrel and independent spirit.

did not replace them for two weeks, Ace did not leave. He prefers his home in the aviary to freedom outdoors. He comes to the opening in the porch each evening to greet me and to see what gifts I bring for his supper. He runs up my arm, around my shoulders, sniffs my ear in greeting, and then dashes back into the aviary with his choice of food. I talk to him as I put other bits of food on his feeding platform.

In the moonlight I can watch him romp among the jungle-gym of limbs around the top of the aviary.

Occasionally, he leaves the aviary in the evening when I feed him and makes an exploring romp across the porch and through the house. But his choice is to spend his time in the aviary.

He is getting plump in his old age, but he is still very quick and active. He helps us by introducing other flying squirrels to the routine of life in the aviary, and offers them company as long as they stay.

Most move right into his nest house with him, although other nest houses are available. Ace shares his food storehouse with them for as long as they are there. When they leave, he settles back into his old routine.

We all like old Ace and respect his choice. He can stay as long as he desires, for he is one of our friends.

:7:
Three Barred Owls

The barred owl was brought into the office by Dennis Reese, wildlife officer with the Florida Game Commission. There were two small, bloody spots on her left wing, and she wasn't able to fly. She had obviously been shot with a shotgun.

Barred owls are rather large, about twelve inches tall. They have dark plumage, and in contrast to the yellow-colored eyes of most owls, their eyes are jet black. They are my favorite owl.

There were no bones broken. Although she resisted having me feel and manipulate the wing, she did not attack me with her beak or talons.

After the examination, I placed her in a cardboard box for the ride home from the office. When I opened the box on the back porch, the big black eyes looked up at me. As I moved, she blinked the blue protective third eyelids that owls have and softly "popped" her beak. The sound is similar to the snapping of fingers, but sharper and more brittle. It is a warning!

I put on heavy gloves. Then, talking quietly, I moved my hand toward her until the back of my hand touched her legs and chest. Still talking to her, I increased the pressure of my hand against her legs. She either had to move backward or step up on my hand.

As if she had been trained to it for years, she stepped gently onto my hand. Slowly and carefully I carried her to a large cage with a comfortable perch in it.

Sliding my hand under the perch until her legs were pressed against it, I repeated the procedure and she stepped onto the perch. Still talking to her, I told her I would feed her in a little while. She blinked her eyelids at me, as if carrying on her half of the conversation.

I kept my promise to her. In an hour I brought her several small pieces of beef heart. Holding a piece in a pair of forceps, I offered it to her. After warning me by popping her beak, she allowed me to touch the piece of meat to her beak. I hoped she would be aggressive enough to bite at it. I touched the hairlike guard feathers beside her beak with the piece of meat. She would not bite. No matter how I moved it about her beak, she would not bite.

Since she was docile and not fighting, I took the meat from the forceps and gently pushed the point of the forceps between the beak at the corner of her mouth and forced her beak open a little ways. I quickly pushed the piece of meat into the mouth with my fingers and moved back a step to watch her. Because she was to prove so gentle, dainty, and feminine in her actions, we later named her The Lady.

She stared at me unblinkingly with the piece of beef heart dangling from her beak. A minute or two later the

"The Lady"

juices seemed to reach her taste buds, and finally she seemed to realize it was food. A quick flip of her head brought the meat into her mouth, where two lesser flips made it disappear as she swallowed. I offered her another piece, which she ignored. But she didn't resist as much when I forced her beak open a second time and placed the meat between its sharp edges.

She held this piece for a few seconds, then it too disappeared. Each successive feeding was easier. By the following day she was reaching for the piece of meat. She had learned to eat quickly.

All our barred owls learn quickly and are gentle.

She was moved to a temporary flight cage at the end of the porch. It was large enough for her to fly from perch to perch. She used the wing some now, and was eating ravenously.

No longer was she content to stay in the cage. Each night, as soon as darkness fell, she would find some way out of the cage. When she escaped from her cage, she was quite content to be free on the porch. She resented being returned to her cage. When she saw me coming to put her back, she would puff up all her feathers to make herself look larger, blink her blue third eyelids, and pop her sharp beak repeatedly and angrily. However, she never tried to bite as she stepped up on my hand, and she never clutched me hard with her talons. She fussed all the way back to her cage each and every time.

If she were free on the porch and I approached her with food in my hand, she never fluffed up or popped. She knew the difference and what each approach meant.

When her flight cage was rendered escape-proof, she was confined for a day, but then she began to pace at evening. She would climb up the side of the cage trying to find some way to escape. Since she could fly some now, I was afraid she might hurt herself. I felt it was time to set her free.

At suppertime I fed her, and then I opened the outside door of the flight cage, giving her a way to freedom.

She sat in the doorway through sundown, and when darkness arrived, she sailed off on noiseless wings.

Not all barred owls are as gentle as The Lady. All seem to have more than just bird intelligence.

Bardol was brought to the house by three young boys from a nearby community. They had found the big owl in the woods.

There wasn't a lot I could do to help him. His right wing had been shattered at the shoulder and was just hanging by a few shreds of tissue. All I could do was remove the damaged wing and close the gaping wound that was left. Bill held the owl gently and kept its head covered with an old bath towel. The owl scarcely moved, and did not try to bite or claw at us as the few sutures were quickly placed.

When it was all over, we put the owl in the bird flight cage at the end of the porch. A few hours later we offered him some strips of beef heart. He was hungry and learned to eat very quickly.

That night I placed four more strips of meat on the perch beside him, and in the morning they were gone.

Now it was simple to feed him. The strips of beef heart covered with the vitamin-mineral powder were placed on his perch in the evening. He ate whatever we offered.

When we saw him taking a bath in his water dish, we knew he was feeling good again. But what can you do with a one-winged owl? Zoos don't want them. They don't make attractive specimens. Certainly they can't get along in the wild. This question began to nag at us.

Each evening now the big owl tried to get out. He climbed the side of the cage and tried to fly with his one good wing. Each attempt ended in a crash landing at the bottom of the six-foot-high flight cage.

Rather than let him hurt himself, we decided to let him stay out one night. I fed him at dusk and left the cage door open. He ate, then sat quietly looking at me. As long as I stood there, he wasn't going to make his escape attempt.

When I checked the cage at bedtime, he was gone. I heard a little rustling noise in the small oak tree near the corner of the house. At first, I couldn't see anything. When I looked more closely I could make out the shape of an owl on a limb. The moonlight, broken and shattered as it passed through the leafy canopy above him, camouflaged him perfectly.

As I shined the flashlight on him, he blinked his big eyelids and popped his beak two times in greeting. He was happy. He was free. His whole appearance radiated contentment as he looked down at me.

I went into the house to report to the rest of the family. "Barred owl is in the little oak tree, and he is enjoying his freedom," I said.

"That's his name," said Bill. "If you say barred owl fast, it sounds like 'Bardol,' that stuff they advertise on TV." This owl was called Bardol from then on.

In the morning before I went to work, I went out and looked for Bardol. He wasn't in the oak tree. In the woods north of the house I heard the blue jays fussing. They don't like owls, so maybe they had found Bardol for me. Sure enough, there he sat two feet above the ground on

Bardol

a low branch of a scraggly pine, being harassed by a crowd of jays. He was not afraid of me as I approached, and he stepped willingly on the short stick offered to him as a perch. I carried him back to his cage, and he hopped into it without any argument.

He was content all day, and in the evening we repeated the same procedure. In the morning I found him again and brought him back. On the way back to his cage we had a little discussion.

"Bardol," I said, "I don't have time to look for you each morning, so if you promise to stay close by the house somewhere, I will let you stay outside all the time. Just be where I can find you in the evening so you can get some food." He listened attentively and blinked his eyes at me several times.

I wasn't really sure if he agreed to our arrangement, but it certainly would be easier on both of us if it worked. Then there would be a place for a one-winged owl, for we didn't mind feeding him.

When I fed him and opened his cage that evening, I reminded him of our morning conversation. As he ate and then stood in the door of the cage, it was obvious he was looking forward to his night of freedom.

In the morning I heard the blue jays, so I knew where he was; but I didn't go after him. That evening the boys and I built a feeding platform ten feet up in an oak tree at the edge of the lawn. We hung a small pail full of water near the platform where he could reach it. After we put food on the platform, we set out to find Bardol. It took about an hour, because this time we didn't have the blue jays to lead us to him. He was near the top of a big oak.

Bill climbed the tree with a short branch for a perch tucked into his belt. But when he got near him, the big owl tried to fly from him and awkwardly fluttered to the ground near us. He was unhurt and let me pick him up.

We took him to the tree where we had built the feeding platform. I placed him on the tree trunk which leaned slightly. He grasped the trunk with his talons. Then, using his good wing to balance himself as a tightrope walker uses an umbrella, he walked up the nearly vertical trunk. Our one-winged owl had taught himself to climb trees.

He found his food on the platform at once. While we watched, he ate and drank. Then he contentedly settled for a nap on the branch beside the feeding platform.

When we went to the house, we knew Bardol was going to be all right. He would make it.

For a year and a half Bardol lived in the trees around the lawn. He moved through most of the trees in the yard, but usually stayed in one of the trees near his feeding platform. He came and ate each night. He seemed content, and we enjoyed hearing his soft hooting in the woods at night. It was Bardol that taught us how adaptable owls can be.

The Traveler was another amazing barred owl. He earned his name. He too was brought into the office with a compound wing fracture. While the ends of the bone were exposed and dirty, the circulation was intact and it was probable that the fractured bones would heal.

The owl was given an anesthetic by injection. As soon as he went to sleep I scrubbed and cleaned his wound, placed a steel pin through the fractured bone, applied antibiotics to the wound, sutured it closed, and then taped the wing to his side in a normal resting position. He was given an injection of antibiotics, and I took him home.

He slept all the way. At home, when he was thoroughly awake, we put him in the big flight cage. He accepted food from my hand at once. He was hungry and ate well. He also immediately learned to take food from the perch, so feeding was not a problem.

Traveler

In a week he felt fine and the wing was healing well. Then it happened! I forgot to lock the cage door after changing his water.

In the morning the owl was gone. I could have kicked myself. There was no way that poor owl could survive with his wing taped to his side. He could not free himself even if it were healed. He appeared to be doomed.

Two weeks later, I received an unusual call at the office.

The Bentleys called, because they knew I worked with wild birds and animals. And they wondered if I knew who had an owl with a bandaged wing.

Excitedly I told them he was staying with us until his wing was healed, but that he had disappeared. I drove right out to pick him up.

When I got there the big owl was standing on the front lawn waiting for me. Like a tired, dignified, little old man, he stood and looked up at me when I spoke to him. He let me pick him up. I thanked the Bentleys for calling me as I carried him to the car.

On the way home I measured the distance the owl had walked. By road it was 1.5 miles. He had walked through fields and orange groves. He had crossed two highways and several yards. He had probably not walked a direct route, so there is no way of knowing how far he had actually traveled.

Once home I offered him some water, then handed him bits of beef heart, which he ate ravenously. Finally he had had enough. He climbed up onto the perch in the corner of the big owl cage and went to sleep at once.

Everyone was glad to see he was back, and we all agreed his name should be The Traveler. By all rights, this should be the end of the story. But a week later he was gone again.

I had changed all his bandages, and the wing appeared to be healing well. He was put back in the big owl cage, but the following day, the door was accidentally left open for only a few moments but long enough to allow The Traveler to disappear again.

For the next three days I listened for blue jays and crows, hoping they would lead me to the owl. No such luck.

We were fortunate to have found him the first time. To expect another miracle was hoping for too much. After a week went by, I felt we had lost him for good.

Each morning when I get up I look out the window, through the aviary, and check the deer and other animals I can see from our bedroom window.

Then, some days later when I looked out the window in the morning, there, standing in the deer pen at the corner of the aviary, was a barred owl with his wing in a sling looking up at me. The Traveler had returned. This time he had found his way back by himself.

Once again he was placed back in the cage and fed till he was satisfied. The gate was securely latched, and it stayed that way until the pin and bandage were removed from the wing.

Each owl is different and unique, but the barred owls seem to understand we are trying to help them, and, in their quiet, dignified way, accept this help graciously.

:8:
Joe Nathan, *a Seagull*

Barbara, Bill, John, and I had been camping in Alaska, our largest state, for a month. We were on the highway near Seward, heading home to central Florida after the month of camping when we saw a swirling mass of white and gray feathers the size of a volleyball just miss being hit by an old blue pickup truck and go rolling along the pavement and into a ditch at the side of the road.

Bill yelled, and we slowed down to stop. Before the camper could come to a full stop, the boys dashed out and an instant later were back again carrying a wet, bedraggled, dirty-gray lump of feathers that had once been a sleek seagull.

As John presented me with the sad-looking package we all saw the badly damaged wing. The boys have unlimited faith in me and felt, since I am a veterinarian, I should be able to fix it at once. Unfortunately the left wing was not only fractured. The broken tip was mutilated and cold—which meant it was beyond repair. "It will have to come off, boys," was the only solution I could offer them. We all knew that this was not a solution for the bird, since there is no place in nature for a gull that can't fly.

We took care of the medical part of the problem.

Two quick snips of Barbara's scissors and the dead tissue was removed without pain or blood. An antibiotic ointment was applied.

Bill placed a large plastic wastebasket on its side, lined it with clean newspaper, and slid our patient tail first into the nest so he could look out. The exhausted bird cocked his head and watched us with an alert eye as we contemplated his fate.

Since both boys had just read *Jonathan Livingston Seagull*, this was temporarily Jonathan. Since we already had a John in the camper, often called Jonathan, the name was quickly changed to Joe Nathan to avoid confusion.

As we continued on our way we discussed our problem and concluded that he would come back to Florida with us and live on our lake, where we could see that he would receive food and care. This meant traveling six-thousand miles with a sick seagull, passing through U.S. and Canadian customs several times, an eight-hundred-mile ferry trip, and all the other unknown factors of care if the seagull were to survive.

After two hours of travel our companion almost looked like a gull again. His feathers had dried, and with the plucky determination characteristic of this gull, he began to preen and straighten his feathers. From the bird book we identified him as a mew gull.

I suggested that the boys see if he were ready to eat. John got the bread, Bill got a shallow bowl and some milk. "It's not seagull chow, but it's the best we can do, Joe," said Bill as he slowly and gently eased the bowl into position in front of the wild bird.

Joe Nathan gave us that beady look which we were to come to know so well and, with the grace of an aristocrat, daintily picked the pieces from the milk and swallowed them. It was clear that he was ravenous. It was equally clear, since he would eat for us, that the first plateau in the successful battle for the life of this bird had been reached.

More permanent quarters had to be prepared, so at the next crossroads town we stopped. For his home, we scrounged a wooden apple box from the trash heap behind a grocery store. To line the bottom of the box and keep it clean, John purchased a box of large disposable baby diapers. It was his idea and his contribution from his spending money. Bill purchased some dry cat chow—fish flavor—and a can of high-protein dog food.

Lined with the baby diaper and some sweet clover pulled from the roadside for a bed, the box was prepared with a bowl of fresh water in one corner and assorted food in the other. Our new member of the family was ready to travel.

He was an agreeable traveler. He voiced no complaints about route or scenery and seemed to enjoy whatever food was offered.

We selected a campground with Joe Nathan in mind

Joe Nathan in his new home, and Bill.

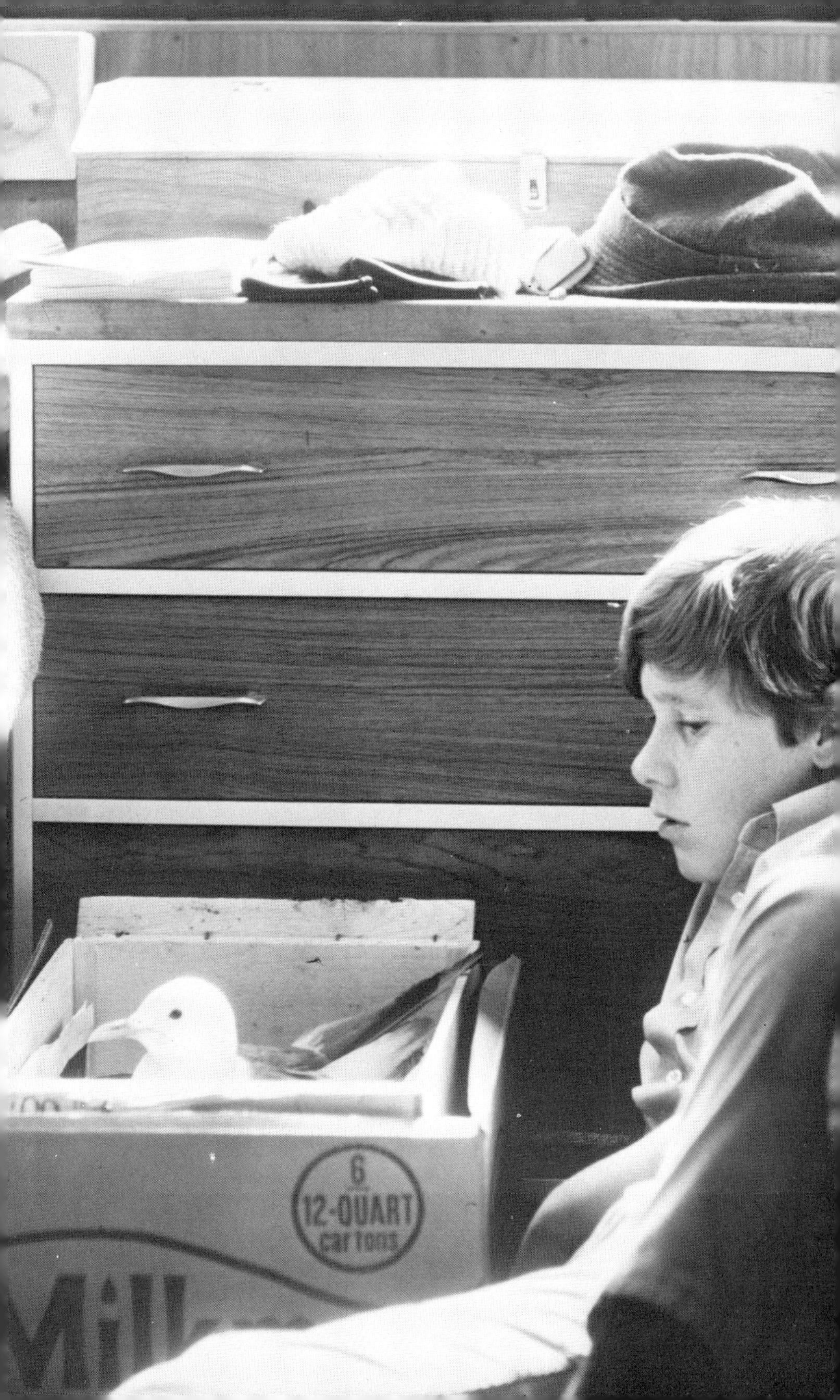
6
12-QUART
cartons

that evening. Bill's specifications were that it had to have a pond or creek where Joe could bathe, but not escape, since he was unable to care for himself.

The second National Forest campground we stopped at met these specifications. The boys took Joe to the water, where he wiggled to escape and then plunged eagerly into the water. Unbalanced by his missing wing he fell on his side, but gaining his balance, he bravely swam to the center of the creek.

He tried to bathe with some success, but when he tried to shake, he toppled sideways. Bill rescued him and brought him back to the campsite. We herded him to the area near the fireplace, where he tried to fly and fell. I debated if it might be more humane to destroy him, but he was intelligent and learned so fast that I didn't want to be the one to snuff out this bright spirit.

After fifteen minutes he learned how far he could wander without being herded by the boys. He recognized these invisible barriers and respected them here and at all future campsites we were to share.

At our bedtime, we put him in his clean box and brought it inside the camper. At six in the morning Joe thumped about on the wooden sides of his box until Bill got up and fed him some moistened cat chow while we all sleepily watched from our beds. Once fed, he settled down and let us sleep a little longer.

When we got up we took him outside and turned him loose so we could clean his box. He immediately ran to the free area he had discovered the night before. He didn't stray while we ate breakfast, but preened and groomed himself until it was time to start off.

After a short chase, he was in his traveling box and ready to spend the day sight-seeing. Twice during the morning we stopped for Joe Nathan's brunches. He ate well and rested comfortably on his sweet clover bower.

He did not like to be handled, as is true of any wild creature, but all other human contacts he accepted with calmness and dignity. Each time he was placed in his box it required a short chase, but once in the box he was a good traveler.

The next night we could find no pond for Joe to swim in. When loosed from his box he ran to the other side of the outdoor fireplace, shook thoroughly, and began to preen. He remembered the routine of the night before. Only once did he start to wander toward the woods, but John's vocal, "Joe Nathan, come back now," made him return to his spot. While we ate supper in the camper, he wandered about the campsite. He was a veteran camper and was turning out to be an easier companion than I had expected or hoped for.

That night, when Bill had to catch him again to bring him in, Joe Nathan bit him on the nose. Bill had bent down to apologize to him for having to catch him and Joe Nathan gave him a reprimand bite.

Once in his box, however, he settled right down into the routine of evening camping and appeared to be happy. Only Bill, with his sore nose, was unhappy.

We stopped the next night at a forest service campground along the highway. We hoped to find a stream or pond there for Joe Nathan to swim in, but no such luck. There was a river, but it was wide and fast. If Joe Nathan got in there he would be in the Bering Sea before long.

Joe is not interested in bathing in three inches of dirty water.

We found a rather large and deep puddle near one of the campsites, so we took that site as a compromise. Joe walked around the puddle, inspected it, then walked back toward the outdoor fireplace. He was not interested in bathing in three inches of dirty water.

His walking about had attracted the attention of a mew gull who had already staked out this campsite as his territory. Screaming loudly, the gull landed beside the puddle. Afraid to venture too close to us, he stood on tiptoe, opened his beak wide, and tried to drive Joe Nathan off with his voice. In no uncertain terms he wanted it understood this was his territory.

But our plucky gray traveler was not intimidated. Joe

Nathan rose to his feet and walked toward the argumentative resident.

John called after him, saying, "Joe Nathan, you had better come back here, that gull will get you." Head down, Joe Nathan trudged on ahead toward the other gull. John couldn't stand it. He took off after Joe Nathan, and as he did so, the local gull flew off and landed in a nearby treetop.

Taking credit for putting the other gull to flight, Joe Nathan raised his head, stood tall, and shook himself thoroughly. In gull language it was obvious that he said, "Well, I sure took care of that bigmouth, didn't I?"

Successful in combat, he started back toward his fireplace post. As John returned to the camper, the local resident gull returned to the ground near the puddle. Heaping loud verbal abuse on Joe Nathan, he strutted as close as he dared to the camper.

Joe Nathan couldn't resist the challenge. He started for the intruder again, and with John's help, again put the intruder to flight.

For the third time Joe Nathan was challenged by the gull, but this time he didn't get John's help. John decided, since the bird wouldn't listen, that he should find out for himself the danger involved. As Joe Nathan approached the stranger, a ritual dance took place. The stranger danced toward Joe Nathan on tiptoe with his neck stretched high and his beak open—calling all kinds of names. Joe Nathan, for his part, trudged silently toward the stranger with his head down, beak almost touching the ground.

At six inches apart, they surveyed each other for some

Joe Nathan, mew gull, proud though minus a wing.

seconds, then came together with a bump. Poor Joe Nathan, unbalanced by the loss of his wing, was knocked over in the first assault. The stranger was all over him in the few seconds it took John to get to them and rescue Joe Nathan. "I told you so, you dumb bird. Didn't I tell you? You just don't have good sense," he kept telling him as he gently smoothed his feathers and carried him back to his spot by the fireplace.

Our gray-white bird was now dusty brown from his roll in the dust and in need of a bath.

The boys decided to take John's pan—purchased for panning gold—and use it for a bathtub for Joe Nathan. They dug a slight depression in the ground, where the pan could rest securely, then filled it with water carried in their mother's teakettle. They had drawn a bath "fit for a gull."

They carried Joe Nathan to it, placed him in the center of the shallow twenty-inch pan, and released him. For a minute he waved his wing and started to run as if to escape. Almost at once he seemed to realize he was in clean water.

He paused, looked about him, dipped his beak in, and took a taste. Seeming to find it acceptable, he took a big drink, then another, then flipped a little water into the air. He immersed his head quickly, then shook his head and neck. Then he squatted and allowed the water to penetrate the dense feathers as he wallowed and shook, spraying water everywhere.

In five minutes, a wet, but clean, bedraggled bird stepped out of the gold pan. He went back to his station and began to preen.

Although the enemy flew by a couple more times taunting him, Joe acted as if he couldn't see or hear him.

As he preened, the boys talked over how well the gold pan had worked, and we agreed that the rest of the way home we could select our campgrounds for our traveling convenience rather than a site where Joe Nathan could bathe.

That evening the supper conversation focused on the

problem that was nagging at all of us. We would have to go through both Canadian customs and U.S. customs several times. Would they allow us to keep Joe Nathan? We did the worrying. Joe Nathan himself seemed unconcerned about the future.

Two days later our veteran traveler and we were face to face with our worry. We agreed to tell the truth if we were asked about pets. Joe Nathan would have to be dependent upon the good will of the customs authorities for both his further traveling and his life.

The first test at U.S. customs on leaving Alaska proved to be no test at all. We were waved on with only the statement, "Stop at Canadian customs twenty miles down the road." Now we had twenty miles' worth of worrying to do instead of having it over with at once.

As we slowed for the Canadian customs office, a uniformed customs officer strode into the road. He stepped to my window and began asking questions.

"Where are you from?"

"Florida."

"How many are in your party?"

"Four."

"Are you all citizens of the United States?"

"Yes."

"What is your destination?"

"Haines, and the Alaskan ferry."

"Do you have any pets?"

There it was, the question we hoped he wouldn't ask. He looked me in the eye.

"Well, not really," I said, "but we do have a bird. He's lost a wing and we want to take him south where he has a chance to survive the winter."

He laughed and said, "That's great, all the way to Florida. Well, if you're collecting birds, there's a raven around here you can take also."

We heaved a collective sigh of relief. Thanking the customs man, we headed south. This successful encounter gave us encouragement for the next border scrutiny.

At Haines, we racked up two more successes, then camped several days more waiting for space on the big ocean-going ferry that would take us south to Prince Rupert, British Columbia. Campground routine was well established for the family, and our gray-backed gull fit in perfectly with his cheerful adaptability. John's gold pan, the bathtub, was kept full, and Joe Nathan bathed, preened, ate, and loafed with us at our campsite.

There was one close call, when a German shepherd wandered through the campsite, threatening Joe Nathan. The gull ran squalling at the top of his lungs toward us. The crisis was soon averted by the boys moving quickly between the gull and the dog. The incident drove home the awareness that Joe recognized us as security and not as a threat any longer.

We finally got our space on the ferry. The trip down the Alaskan coast lasted two nights and a day. Passengers were allowed to visit their vehicles only while the ship was docked. This meant that at each of the six stops the boys would have to race below decks, change Joe's box, give him fresh food and water, and reassure him that he was not abandoned.

On the third trip belowdecks Bill noticed that Joe Nathan wasn't eating as he should. On the fourth trip we all went down to check. Joe had stopped eating altogether. He was sick. From what little we could see in the dim light, it appeared to be an intestinal infection. We found some penicillin capsules in our first-aid kit, and I showed Bill how to open them, discard most of the contents, and make a bird-dose capsule.

Joe was given a capsule at each of the remaining stops. But he still wasn't eating when we disembarked. We stopped in Prince Rupert to rest and sight-see, but before we left, we let Joe out for some exercise and a bath. He took a couple of sips of his bath water, then just sat drooped beside his pan. He didn't preen, shake, or eat—he was sick!

We added a portion of a vitamin to his penicillin capsule, but he still wasn't eating. The next day we visited a salmon cannery. The boys talked our guide into giving them several small pieces of fresh salmon "for our seagull." Even these tasty bits were refused by the sick bird.

The following day, Bill spent a great deal of the travel time sitting by the box talking to the quiet gray gull trying to get him to eat. He offered a variety of foods, from fresh grapes to salmon. Finally Joe drank a little milk and ate two tiny pieces of bread. We were encouraged, but he didn't eat anything more all day.

The following day, as we were nearing the U.S. border at Idaho, he seemed to perk up considerably. He ate a couple of grapes, a little dog food, and a little bread and milk.

We found we could make the U.S.-Canada border that evening if we kept on driving. We decided to try for it. We had two more customs hurdles. We all felt the same way. We wanted to get the suspense over with. If we were passed, we had a clear trip to Florida and home.

Joe Nathan, *a Seagull* : 135

Joe Nathan was the least concerned of the group as we approached the Canadian customs office. As we slowed to stop, the officer stepped into the doorway and waved us on. He wasn't even going to stop us. One down, and one more to go.

Farther down the road we stopped beside the U.S. customs officer who was waiting for us. He looked at all of us intently, then told us to have a good trip and waved us on.

It was a happy family that camped in Idaho that night.

When we crossed most of Montana the following day Joe was almost himself again. He was interested in what we were doing and watched us with those intent beady eyes. When he tried to take a bath in his drinking water, we knew he was almost well again.

The following day we crept across the map toward our home in Florida. Our traveler was himself again, and we were all much more cheerful now that he was better.

Crossing the states of the Deep South, Joe stoically endured the heat. When he became too hot during the middle of the day, he would stand with his wing drooped and his mouth open, panting. The boys placed ice cubes in his drinking water to help cool him down, and twice a day let him bathe in the gold pan filled with water and ice cubes, which he relished.

The remaining states were traversed without incident, and one night after midnight we pulled into our own yard and home. We placed Joe and his box on the back porch for the night, and a tired family tumbled into bed.

In the morning, long before I was ready to get up, I heard a pounding at the lakeshore. Bill and John were already up and constructing a temporary pen for Joe Nathan. The plan was to hold him in the pen for a few days and give him time to adapt, then to allow him the freedom of the lake.

Joe Nathan seemed to sense the boys' excitement. He kept standing on tiptoe in his box and peering intently toward the lake. The pen was finished, and Joe was carried to the water in his box. We all went along to see Joe Nathan's reaction.

Bill lifted him gently from the box and set him on a sandy strip at the water's edge. Joe Nathan paused, cocked his head at us, gave us the beady eye, as if to ask why he was getting all the attention, then calmly walked into the water.

He swam completely around the pen, checking out the wire perimeter thoroughly. Then he bathed. He seemed completely relaxed. When he came to shore and began to preen, he seemed to be very much at home.

:9:
The Friendly Otter

His once shiny fur was rumpled and oil-smeared and his eyes were closed. He whimpered softly as he lay on the examination table. The young otter had been hit trying to cross a busy highway. The driver tried to avoid him, but struck him solidly enough to send him tumbling into the roadside grass.

The driver took an old towel and folded it around the still body. He brought it to our office to see if the otter could be helped. My partner, Dr. Jones, shares my interest in wildlife, and he examined the otter at once. The otter had a severe concussion. All his vital signs were all right, but the blow to the head meant he would not regain consciousness for several hours to several days.

The little otter never moved as several injections were given. Then he was placed in a cage where he could be kept quiet.

All that day and the next, the little otter never moved. Except for his regular breathing he appeared to be dead.

There was no movement even when he received injections to feed him and to treat the concussion.

The following day he began to show signs of coming back. Noises caused him to raise his head, but there was no sign that he saw anyone as he turned his dull, glazed eyes toward the sound. Now when he received an injection to feed him, he feebly tried to move away from the pain of the needle. He was coming back.

The next day he drank liquids that were trickled cautiously into his mouth. His eyes were brighter, as they focused on the people who talked to him and were trying to help him. He made no attempt to bite, but did crawl to the far corner of his cage to escape the strange creatures.

Each day he improved. Now he could stand, walk unsteadily, and was eating solid food as well as drinking liquids from a bowl. As soon as he walked without wobbling, I planned to take him home and turn him loose in our lake.

This was easier said than done. The little otter looked soft, cuddly, and gentle; but he was still a wild animal. He had to be moved without hurting him or us. While he wasn't aggressive, I had seen the wounds a savage otter can make. A fellow veterinarian had been treating an otter when it turned, and, with its powerful jaws, took a piece of flesh the size of a half-dollar from his hand. As I looked at the little otter, I reminded myself that it took two months for that hand to heal. All wild creatures have to be treated with respect, for they have the ability to retaliate when frightened or hurt.

The most practical way to move him, we decided, was to trap him and confine him. When he entered the trap to get the tuna fish cat food which we used as bait, he would step on a treadle that would close the door behind him.

The otter was used to seeing people close to his cage. Their presence represented food. Trustingly he entered the box trap as soon as it was placed in his cage. The door swung closed behind him. We had our otter and headed for home.

When we got there John and I went into the deer pen, down to the pond, and opened the trap. The otter looked out at us, but stayed inside the trap.

While he peered out at us, John went to get some more tuna. I dragged a log to the water's edge, so he could have a spot to rest on out of the water.

He watched all these preparations from the trap, but he was much more interested in the water than the food. In a moment he walked out of the trap and went to the water's edge. He tested it, then gracefully slid into the water like butter off a hot knife.

He swam underwater six feet and then came to the surface. He looked at us, dived again, and swam from one side of the pond to the other. He was enjoying himself. After a twenty-minute swim, he came to the shore, crawled out on the bank, and began grooming his thick coat.

It appeared that otter was fine and adapting well. John and I picked up the trap and went back to the house.

At lunch, we could look out the kitchen window and see the otter swimming and grooming himself. Finally he entered the high grass at the edge of the pond and disappeared. We hoped it was just to take a nap.

Later in the afternoon I saw the little otter again diving and swimming in the pond. I took some food down

The otter looked at us and dived again.

to him, but he ignored it as he had the food we had placed on his log. He came out of the water several times, but only for a moment, then began swimming and diving again. Later in the afternoon he was gone again.

When we saw him the next time, the setting sun had turned the pond surface into shimmering gold. His black head caused little gold ripples each time he came to the surface. We enjoyed watching both the otter and the pond in the evening sunset.

Then I noticed something was not right. The otter came

The Friendly Otter : 141

up on the shore a little way and then half-rolled and half-fell back into the water. He swam ten feet, crawled up on shore, and fell back into the water. Then he swam to the middle of the pond, stopped, lifted his head well above the surface, looked about him, and then sank straight down. When he struggled to the surface, he coughed, and water gushed from his mouth and throat.

The otter was drowning.

I started for the porch door calling to John to bring the box. I grabbed a Styrofoam float and another box. John was close behind me.

When we got to the shore the otter had reached the south edge of the pond. He was moving along the shore toward where we stood on the east side. He would go a foot up on shore, fall back into the water, swim six feet, walk into the shallow water for a couple of feet, and then crawl out on shore again. He acted blind, drunk, and dazed as he struggled toward us.

I stepped into the water to intercept him. I knew if he went into deep water, we would lose him. He was too weak to make it. I put the float up as a barricade to block his path, while John placed his box nearby. If the otter traveled along the barricade trying to find a way around it, he would walk right into the box. John and I stood motionless so as not to frighten him as he staggered toward us. When the otter came even with us, he bumped into the float, which forced him closer to shore. I kept it firmly against him, forcing him toward John and the cardboard box. Neither of us spoke. We didn't want to do anything to frighten him. As he staggered through the shallow water, I nudged him closer and closer to the box.

In another moment we had him. The instant he was inside the box, John tipped it up and we closed the lid. We both gave a big sigh of relief.

The otter hadn't eaten since we turned him loose. Evidently he wasn't completely well yet. He had swum himself into exhaustion.

We put the box in the large aviary cage at the corner of the house. We turned the box on its side and opened the top but the otter didn't come out. It was almost completely dark now, and as we peered inside there was just enough light to see that the otter was lying on his side. He was very still. I nudged him cautiously, but he didn't move. We let him rest and checked him again a few minutes later.

He was still the same, but when we checked him again he was worse. He was convulsing. His feet pedaled aimlessly, his jaws quivered, and saliva dripped from his lips. It looked as if he had reinjured his head, as if the hemorrhage in the brain from the original concussion had started again. There wasn't anything we could do now to help except keep him warm and comfortable.

John and I were depressed as we walked back into the house. When I checked the otter later that night, he appeared to be in a deep coma. Occasionally he would twitch slightly or whimper softly, but otherwise he was completely still. I was certain he would be dead by morning.

In the morning I went out to the aviary, picked up the box, and carried it to my car. I planned to take the otter's body to the office and prepare it and a report for the state diagnostic laboratory. We needed to know what went wrong and the exact cause of death.

The Friendly Otter : 143

I don't know what made me decide to inspect the otter one last time. When I opened the top and peered into the box, a whiskered face with black shiny eyes peered back at me.

I called to John and Barbara and took the otter and the box back to the aviary. The little otter hadn't moved when I had picked up the box and carried it to my car, but now the box literally danced in my hands as he bounced around.

Once in the aviary, I placed some canned dog food in the food dish, while John filled a plastic dishpan with water for a water dish and swimming pool. Then we turned the box on its side, opened the lid, stepped out of the aviary quickly, and closed the door.

In just a second the whiskered face peeped out of the box. He appeared happy to see us. A wisp of dog food odor reached his nose. He sniffed twice, then quickly went to the food dish and ate ravenously.

We smiled, watching him eat with much lip smacking and contented gurglings. Not good table manners, but we were happy to see him feeling better. What's more, he seemed just as happy to see us.

We decided to keep him in the aviary for another week. Then we would try to release him again. The cardboard box would be his temporary house, we would feed him three times daily, and we would keep his swimming pool dishpan filled with clean water.

That first day he slept and ate, but was not active. He prepared a nest in one corner of the aviary and slept there most of the time.

Each time I brought food, he would see me coming and

dance toward the door to meet me. He cavorted more like a young puppy than a wild otter. He never growled or acted as if he would bite, but gave a little grunting bark in greeting. I put the food in the pan and when he started eating, I entered the pen. He continued to eat but watched my every movement. I emptied his swimming pool and refilled it. Each time I left the aviary he would stop eating, and he would follow me to the door, as if he didn't want me to leave. He actually seemed to enjoy the company and seemed to enjoy my talking to him.

This became our routine for the next week. When I called him or talked to him, he would answer with a little half-grunt half-bark, or he would pick up his food dish and rattle it. He would follow me around the aviary as I cleaned his swimming pool and used a short-handled shovel to clean out the food wastes and bowel material.

As he followed me about, I wasn't certain I could trust him, so I used the shovel as a shield. I held it in front of him to stop him when he got too close, and maneuvered behind it as I cleaned the aviary.

Each day I worried less about his biting me. Now as I went about my chores the little otter was usually beside me watching with interest everything I did. He would come up close and place one foot on my shoe and look up at me as I talked to him. He was gentle. I wanted to pet him, but felt that would be taking too much liberty.

Finally it was time to offer him freedom again. Saturday afternoon John and I opened the aviary door, showed him the food we placed in his food dish, and then started down the hill toward the pond carrying his dish and food.

The little otter hesitated for a few moments at the door,

The Friendly Otter : 145

then started after us with a loping run that made him hump up like an inch worm with each stride. He caught up to us, got under my feet, and we both almost went sprawling.

I gave him one bite of the dog food and while he was eating it, John and I got a head start toward the water. By the time he caught us we were at the water's edge.

The otter sniffed the food, sniffed the water, tasted the water, and then tasted the food. Then, undecided whether to eat or swim, he entered the shallow water, sprawled on the sand with half of his body in the water, reached for the food, and ate.

Afterward, he swam about for a while, then disappeared into the tall grass on the west side of the pond.

He swam about for a while, then disappeared.

We didn't see him the rest of the day.

The aviary is close to our bedroom window. That night at bedtime, just as I turned off the light I heard a noise at the aviary door. I went to the window and listened. There was a scratching and thumping at the aviary door. I got my flashlight and went to the porch where I could see the door.

When I turned on the flashlight there was the whiskered otter smiling at me. He wanted back into his sanctuary— his home. He grunted twice when I spoke to him. I called to Barbara. She came to look at the otter that wanted to go back into his pen.

I must confess to a tremendous feeling of satisfaction. Here was a truly wild creature with whom we had established a bond of trust that was strong enough that he was willing to give up freedom to come back with us. I guess this is the reason you get "hooked" on helping these wild creatures.

I opened the gate on the aviary and the otter went in. He went over to his corner and curled up as if to sleep, but since I was still watching him, he raised his head, cocked his head to one side, and fixed those big black eyes on me. It was as if he were saying, "It's time for bed, don't just stand there—go to sleep."

About that time Barbara came up beside me, bringing a freshly opened can of dog food, thinking he might like a midnight snack.

He watched me as I put some food in his dish. When we got into bed, we could hear him smacking his lips as he ate his snack. We were glad he was back and safe.

The otter woke us up at dawn scratching at the door

of the aviary. He wanted out. I picked up a can of dog food and went out and opened his gate. He didn't come out at once, but stood by his food dish. When I stood there watching him, he looked back at me for a moment, then picked up the aluminum dish and shook it, rattling it against the ground to indicate that he was ready for his breakfast.

As I put food in his dish, he came over, placed a foot on the toe of my shoe, and looked up at me watching my movements. When I finished, he moved off my foot and went to the food dish. I left the gate open and went back to the house for breakfast.

Before I left for work I looked into the aviary. The little otter was gone. We didn't see him all day, but that night about ten-thirty I heard him scratching at the door and making his little grunting-barking noise. I went out, opened the gate for him, fed him, and then locked his gate again.

We could not leave the gate to the aviary open for his convenience. A little flying squirrel lived in a house in an upper corner of the aviary. The raccoon that lived in the woods beside the house had tried to get Ace several times when we had accidentally left the door open. I didn't want the squirrel to end up as a raccoon's meal. So we kept the aviary door closed at night.

We kept it closed in the daytime against gray squirrels and blue jays. They would come into the cage to pick up bits of leftover food, then they would become confused about where they were and race around like addled creatures. Blue jays and squirrels in there together, frightened one another and frantically whirled from spot to spot until they were all thoroughly exhausted. Except when we let the otter in or out, we had to keep the aviary door closed.

This meant a new routine was established. Each night between ten and eleven the otter would come back to the aviary to be let in. I put his dish just outside the door. It was easier to hear him rattling his dish when he wanted in than it was to hear his soft barking noises. When we heard him, I would get the can of dog food and go out, let him in the aviary, and feed him. The otter was always glad to see me and frisked around happily while I prepared his food dish.

I didn't worry about his biting me anymore, but I never tried to pet him or handle him; for we meant for him to go back to the wild and not to keep him as a pet.

In the morning he would scratch at the door and bang his food pan when he wanted to go out. I would get up, go out, open the door, put food in his dish, and place the dish outside the aviary. This morning routine was fine for a while, but then the otter upset the routine.

Originally he got me up each morning a little before seven. This was fine, because I usually woke up about then. But then he started waking me at six-thirty, then at six, and then even earlier. When he woke me at 3 A.M. and wanted out, that was the last straw.

That evening I moved his box and his dishpan-swimming pool outside the aviary. I fixed him a substantial shelter alongside one wall of the aviary and placed his food dish by the gate as usual. When he came in that night about eleven, I tried to explain things to him. "Otter, I am not going to let you in the aviary tonight. Your box,

The Friendly Otter : 149

your water, and everything are right here. I will feed you and then you sleep outside here, so I don't have to get up and let you out in the middle of the night." He stood with one foot on the toe of my shoe and looked up at me as if he understood. I put extra food in his dish, so he would have some left for a morning snack, and went back into the house. "Now if Winky doesn't try to eat him, he should do all right out there," I answered when Barbara asked how the otter liked the new arrangement.

At bedtime Otter barked softly a couple of times when he heard us talking in the bedroom. I spoke to him through the open window and he answered. We slept soundly that night and when we got up in the morning the little otter was gone. We didn't see him in the pond all that day. If he came back that night we would know that he was accepting the new routine.

Right on schedule at ten that night we heard the feed pan rattling. I went out and talked to him as he frisked around my legs. I was glad to see him, and he seemed to feel the same way. I fed him an extra large portion of supper and put some more in for his morning snack.

About midnight I heard him barking and hissing. He had never done that before. I got up and went to the porch with my flashlight. He hissed again. As I put the light first on him and then in the direction of his gaze, there was Winky.

She was standing by the otter's swimming pool-dishpan. Her little paws were searching all over the bottom of the pan of water for food as she gazed at the stars unconcerned by the hissing otter. In a few moments, when her fishing proved futile, she advanced on the little otter protecting its food dish. She snarled at him and made a tentative lunge at the otter, but he would not be intimidated. He stood his ground, opened his mouth to show his sharp teeth, and hissed back at her. They exchanged unpleasantries for a few moments, then the raccoon retreated into the darkness.

We spoke to the otter to reassure him. The little otter looked up at me, grunted happily a couple of times, and curled up to sleep.

In the morning he was gone again by the time we got up. Since we never saw him in the pond during the daytime, it meant he was going back and forth to the lake. He was ranging farther and becoming less dependent upon us.

At the weekend a new dimension was added to the routine. John and I were working in the yard Saturday morning when the otter announced his arrival with a series of happy squeaks and grunts. He apparently heard our voices and left the lake and came to the house. While John stood and talked to him, I went and got his food. He ate happily while we watched and then started down to the pond. He stopped on the way several times and looked back at us as if inviting us to join him, but when we declined he continued to the pond, swam across it, and disappeared in the tall weeds on the other side. He was definitely headed for the big lake.

That night he came back at his usual time, and on Sunday morning he came back to the house for another brief visit.

On Monday, even though John was in school and I was at work, the otter came up to the house. Barbara heard

The Friendly Otter : 151

the barred owl fussing and went to see what had upset him. The otter's happy squeaks and grunts at the back porch door greeted her. She got him some breakfast, and sat and talked to him while he ate. Then he went back to the pond and out to the lake.

Now he came to the house each morning for a visit and a snack. And he still came after dark each night.

I was curious about where the otter was staying in the lake. I took my camera and went down to the shore. The shoreline was so overgrown with heavy weeds that it was necessary to walk in the water to make my way around the lake. As I waded along in knee-deep water, I scanned the shoreline for any sign of the friendly otter. I didn't see him anywhere. I called for him several times. "Otter, otter, where are you, boy?" Every thirty seconds or so I would call loud enough so that my voice would reach into the weeds along the shore where he might be sleeping.

When I was about to give up I saw him. The little otter was swimming toward me. Every ten feet his head popped to the surface, coming closer each time.

As he approached I couldn't help worrying. This was an entirely new situation. The otter expected his people friends to provide him with food. Yet I couldn't feed him in the water; there was no place to set the food down. If he didn't get fed what would he do? Would he become frightened by my splashing as I walked through the thigh-deep water and bite me?

The otter swam right to me. I could feel his little forefeet as he touched my bare legs. He swam up to me, and his bristly whiskers brushed along my legs as he circled them and then swam between them. His little paws patted my ankles and bare calves gently as he pulled himself around my legs. He swam off two or three feet, surfaced, looked at me expectantly, and then dived back between my legs. I dropped a few pieces of dry dog food from my pocket into the water near him. It floated past him, but he ignored it as he frisked between my legs again and again.

After the third or fourth time, I began to relax. It was as if he were welcoming me to come and play. This was his environment, and he was happy to see me here.

I walked slowly toward shore. I tried not to trip over the little otter as I walked to the water's edge. When we got there I spread some of the dry dog food out for him. He sniffed at it, but he didn't eat. He just wanted to play.

I tried to take pictures as he frisked about, but he moved faster than I could focus the camera. I gave it up as a bad job.

We went back into the water and headed for the beach along our yard. I walked slowly and he played around in the water beside me. I moved with confidence through the shallow water while the otter darted about my legs. I kept a regular stride toward the beach, but he was so quick that I never kicked him as he moved under me.

When we got to the beach the otter didn't want to leave the lake to come to the house. I called to John and he brought some canned dog food to the beach. The otter enjoyed this snack, and when he finished eating he swam back along the shoreline to where he established his home.

He didn't want to come back to the house.

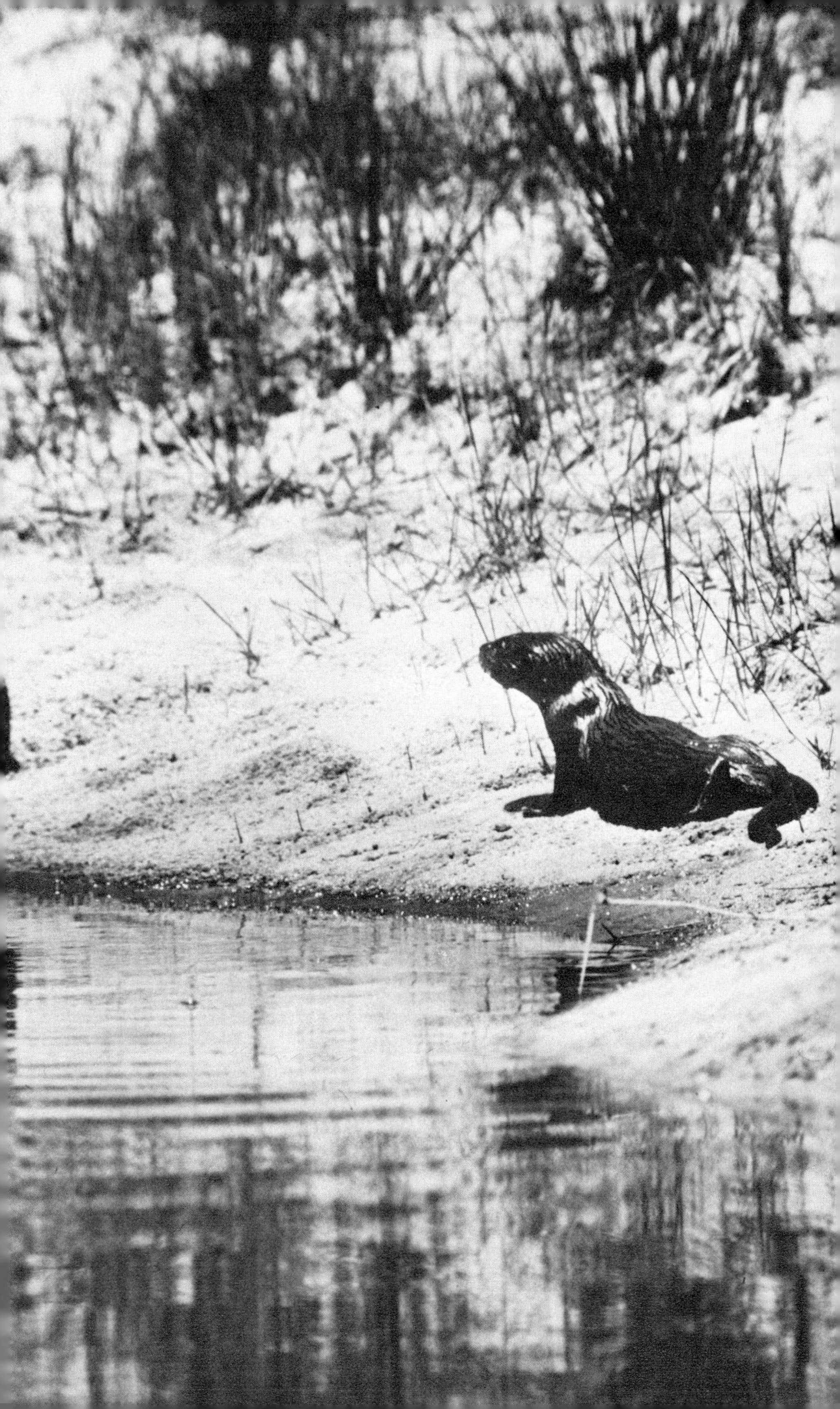

The next evening I went to the lakeshore with the canned dog food and called to him. In a few minutes I saw him swimming toward me. The otter ate and we visited for a few moments, and then he swam back to his spot on the shoreline.

That night he didn't come up to the house at bedtime. Now he was spending the night on the lakeshore. He did come to the house in the morning, when Barbara fed him.

That evening, the otter came to the house again. Since I hadn't gone to the beach and called him, he came to the house looking for me. We visited while I fed him, and he went back to the lake.

Now a new routine was established. The otter came up in the morning to be fed and then came up about six in the evening for his supper. He no longer went to the aviary and rattled his food dish, but came directly to the back door and squeaked and grunted until someone noticed him and fed him. He was getting us well trained. I didn't mind, but I was worried that perhaps he was getting too dependent upon people. Would he ever be able to become a wild otter again?

That next weekend this dependency was partially broken. John and I were cutting firewood near the tool shed in the back yard. Since his brother Bill had gone off to college, John had plenty of "family togetherness" as he and I did the chores together on the weekends.

John's burro is allowed to roam free in the yard when we are working there, instead of being confined to her pasture. She had a rope dangling from her neck, so we could catch her if necessary, but she had the freedom of the yard. She enjoys wandering around grazing and helping us with our chores. She doesn't wander off and comes when John calls her.

The otter made his twice daily trips to the house usually by leaving the lakeshore, traveling three-hundred feet toward the pond, crawling under the deer fence, traveling along the north side of the pond, and heading directly to the porch. At the porch he crawled under the fence again and came to the porch step and the door for food.

John and I were working away from the porch, so when the otter heard our voices he came directly from the lake toward us, not traveling through the deer pen.

Halfway from the shore—in the middle of the lawn—the otter met the burro. When the burro saw the otter, it came charging down on it, curious to see what this creature was. The otter looked so tiny as it cowered before the burro. It must have appeared to the otter that a giant gray monster was pursuing it. Certainly it must have been terrifying. The burro wanted to examine the otter, and as the otter retreated the burro followed it, snorting and sniffing. John and I rushed to rescue the otter. John caught the burro's rope, and we tried to reassure the terrified otter. The little otter started to relax and follow me when John's dog spotted it.

The dog, a black and white border collie, is appropriately named Trouble. She instinctively tries to herd any creature she finds. Barking furiously, she placed herself between the otter and the lake and tried to herd it toward the house. Every move the otter made was instantly countered by the dog. John tied the curious burro to a tree, and dashed back to rescue the otter from Trouble. Obediently Trouble came to his side and followed him to the tool shed, where she, too, was confined.

Hesitantly, the otter followed me to the porch door. I got his food and quietly reassured him as he started to eat. Halfway through the meal, Thomas, a big gray, white, and black tomcat, came around the corner. Before I could interfere, it walked up close to the otter, arched its back, and spit at the otter. That was the final straw.

The little otter looked reproachfully at me, turned, and leaving its food half-eaten, started for the lake. It looked back at me a couple of times as I talked to it, but didn't stop in its determined lope to the security of the big lake.

The little otter never came to the house again. When he didn't show up the next day, I went out into the lake and walked to where I usually found him. He didn't come when I called, but I found that he was living in an abandoned alligator hole in the bank of the lakeshore.

From the fresh signs around the entrance, I knew the otter was eating well. He could find his own food, so his survival was not a worry. But we missed his visits. Two days later, I went back to the lakeshore to check. There were no new signs; the otter had left our area of the lake.

Happy that the otter could get along on his own, but unhappy to have lost our friend, we resigned ourselves to the fact that he was gone. Once again we realized how fragile the bond is between a wild creature and those of us who wish to be their friends.

Two weeks after the otter left, we had a happy surprise. A friend who lives on another lake about one mile east of us and knows of our interest in wildlife stopped Barbara in the grocery store to tell her about an otter. Ann said they were on the beach when this young otter came up to them. It was friendly and squealed happily as it followed them up the lawn from their beach to the house.

It had to be our otter. A quarter mile farther east is Lake Griffin, Florida's second largest lake. The otter is headed in that direction. There are no major highways he has to cross, and the lake has a well-established otter population. In this lake he should be safe.

:10:
Odds and Ends

It should be easy to stop here and to be able to feel that I have told about the major characters we have met. But it is not easy, because there are so many that have not been mentioned.

There was the mockingbird Bodine, raised from a baby, who flew to the car to greet us each time we came home.

There is a mouse named Cactus that lives on the back porch in the woodpile. Several times Cactus has been put outside to be free, but he finds his way back into his woodpile by way of the porthole.

There was Crow Vadis, who taught himself to ride around the yard on the old red dachshund's back. He enjoyed coming into the house to share the warmth of the family each night at suppertime. If we tried to ignore him, he flew from the back of the house to the front of the house, peered in the windows, and uttered the most horrible cries of agony until the door was opened to him. He never asked for food, nor expected to be fed at this

The retarded rabbit who housebroke himself.

time, but rather joined in the conversation with his own vocabulary of squeaks, caws, whistles, and happy gurgles. After supper he wanted to go back outside.

Happily Crow Vadis found a flock of crows that adopted him. He came back to see us regularly all fall, but the following spring he left forever.

There is the retarded rabbit. As a tiny baby in the nest, he was stepped upon by a young giraffe. While he lived and grew well, he was not agile enough to escape from enemies in the wild. He had the freedom of the house and porch. While he carried his head tilted slightly to one side, and hopped sideways when he was in a hurry, he housebroke himself and used a sandpan on the porch for all his eliminations.

There was Bipper, Roach, Goldie, Snick-Snick, the bear cub, and Teddy, the Terrible Tufted Titmouse. There

Teddy, the not-so-terrible titmouse.

were so many creatures that wrote their own stories and were part of our lives.

They have been satisfying, beneficial, and educational for all of us. Certainly my life as a veterinarian has been enriched by the wild orphan friends we have met and shared our home with.